Teach Me—
I Dare You!

**Judith Allen Brough,
Sherrel Bergmann,
and Larry C. Holt**

EYE ON EDUCATION

EYE ON EDUCATION
6 DEPOT WAY WEST, SUITE 106
LARCHMONT, NY 10538
(914) 833–0551
(914) 833–0761 fax
www.eyeoneducation.com

Library of Congress Cataloging-in-Publication Data

Brough, Judith Allen.
    Teach me, I dare you! / Judith Allen Brough, Sherrel Bergmann, and Larry C. Holt.
        p. cm.
    Includes bibliographical references and index.
    ISBN 1-59667-018-5
    1. Motivation in education. 2. Effective teaching. I. Bergmann, Sherrel. II. Holt, Larry C.
    III. Title.
LB1065.B777 2006
370.15′4—dc22

                                                        2005034879

10 9 8 7 6 5 4 3

Editorial and production services provided by
Richard H. Adin Freelance Editorial Services
52 Oakwood Blvd., Poughkeepsie, NY 12603-4112
(845-471-3566)

Also Available from EYE ON EDUCATION

Dedication

To Gordon Vars, Conrad Toepfer, and J. Howard Johnston. We dared them to teach us and they did!

Meet the Authors

Dr. Judith Allen Brough is Chair and Professor of Education at Gettysburg College in Pennsylvania. She has served as a constultant for agencies that are building programs to engage students in their learning. She has interviewed thousands of students and their teachers in various states and countries regarding student interests, motivations, and challenges. She has been recognized for her efforts as a student advocate through several organizations, including the Gruhn/Long/Melton Award from the National Association of Secondary School Principals and the William Alexander Award from the Pennsylvania Middle School Association.

Dr. Sherrel Bergmann has been teaching, counseling, and researching at-risk students and their teachers for over thirty years. As a professor at National Louis University, she taught teachers who face these students in their classrooms everyday. Two of her earlier books, *Discipline and Guidance: The Thin Line in the Middle School*, published by National Association of Secondary School Principals; and *Decision Making Skills for Middle School Students*, published by the National Education Association, have relayed both research results and programmatic suggestions to teachers and administrators. She has consulted with hundreds of school districts, parent groups, and educational associations about students who dare us to teach them. Her work has been recognized with the Lounsbury Award from the National Middle School Association and the Gruhn/Long/Melton Award from the National Association of Secondary School Principals. She is currently writing, consulting, and teaching in northern Michigan.

Dr. Larry C. Holt is an Associate Professor at the University of Central Florida in the Department of Educational Studies. His research interests include general methods, student learning, middle level education, and technology. He has authored two books: *Cooperative Learning in Action*, published by the National Middle School Association and *Instructional Patterns: Strategies for Maximizing Student Learning*, published by Sage. He was a Fulbright scholar to the country of Lithuania 1997 to 1998.

Foreword

We have all had them in our classes. They're actually quite easy to spot. It's the kid who is fast asleep with his head on the desk, the too-mature-looking girl putting on makeup, the quiet boy who draws obsessively in his notebook, the young woman absorbed in a teen-style magazine, the sullen youth who declares to everyone that life sucks. The variety of behaviors that convey their disdain and detachment from school are almost infinite, but the message is always very clear: I don't want to be here... just leave me alone... stay off my back. In short, they are challenging us: "Teach me—I dare you!"

Sadly, the reasons for disengagement are often as diverse as the students themselves, and too often imbedded in the complexities and vicissitudes of contemporary life that are well beyond the control, or even the influence, of the school. Academic problems, family disruptions, poor peer relationships, failed romances, premature sexual activity, drug or alcohol use, and dozens of other conditions can contribute to detachment from school and other high-risk behaviors. But the resulting school behavior is almost always the same: low profile withdrawal, passive but clear manifestations of contempt for school and all of its activities, or overt disruptions that range from clowning around to outright hostility and aggression. Regardless of the behavior, the ultimate outcome is, almost invariably, school failure and a tremendously increased risk for dropping out.

It is easy to be discouraged by these students because they seem to value none of the rewards that schools prize so highly and distribute with ceremony. Similarly, they greet with stoic detachment the normal school sanctions of failing grades, withheld privileges, additional assignments, detentions, suspensions, or even expulsions. Nothing that the school can offer or withhold seems to touch them. In the words of a colleague-principal, working with these kids is like "trying to push a rope through mud." It is a frustrating challenge that school professionals, particularly those in the middle grades, have faced with relatively little success for years, due largely, to lack of information and knowledge about these detached students and the absence of sound, proven strategies for working with them.

With the publication of *Teach Me—I Dare You!* all of that has changed. Teachers and school leaders will all continue to find challenging and detached students in their classrooms, but for the first time, they are now equipped with a clear, explicit, and promising set of strategies and tools for breaking through the barriers of disdain and detachment in order to work with these kids. The authors, all long-time advocates for young adolescents, are talented professionals with deep and continuing connections to schools, offer research-based information and proven interventions for helping these most difficult children succeed in school and ultimately, in life. The book is a life-saver not only for frustrated teachers, but also for students who desperately need adult help but don't know how to ask for it or accept it when it's offered.

Professors Bergmann, Brough, and Holt have taken a systemic and comprehensive view of the problem of student detachment and bring a deep and sympathetic understanding of both the students who suffer from the threat of a diminished future and the dedicated professionals who struggle to teach them. They treat the complexity of issues that produce student apathy as an interlocking and highly interactive system that considers all of the critical variables: academic, social, physical, and organizational. Because of their familiarity with the literature on the vast range of topics that contribute to this problem and the authenticity of their experience with young people, they distill the most essential information from the research and focus on the most critical areas for intervention. In essence, they make the problem understandable and approachable. The book inspires confidence that we can not only understand why students disconnect from school, but also intervene in ways that reconnect them to our schools and to a promising future.

The theme that runs through the work is that all successful interventions are authentic and relationship based. The answers are not to be found in managing ever more complex contingencies, such as rewards, sanctions or "high stakes" policies. Distilled to its essence, the book is about how a community of adults can dedicate itself to the success of all children under their charge, adopt a "whatever it takes" stance to assure that success, and support one another and their students in using the strategies and interventions that are both effective and ethical.

The authors have taken a courageous stance and issued a daunting challenge: schools can and must do something to address one of the most difficult segments of the student population: those who just don't seem to care. More than that, however, they have accepted their own challenge by providing understanding, guidance, compassion, and practical wisdom to those who are dedicated to the century-old ideals of the middle level school, commitments that clearly predate the sometimes silly and transparent rhetoric of contemporary political life—the serious and genuine commitment to leaving no child behind.

J. Howard Johnston
Jamaica, Vermont

Table of Contents

Introduction

Some students don't need us. They seem to be able and willing to learn whatever is thrown their way. Some students need us and seem always to be asking questions or pleading for help. Other students, however, seem not to want us. They exude a disdain for us, for school, for learning. If they come to class, they're unprepared. They doze, they shrug; they seem not to care about anything. Threats don't work; calls home don't work; failing grades don't work. These kids come in all colors, all sizes, all ages, all socioeconomic groups, and both sexes. They're not dumb. They just don't *do* anything. Why is that? What can we do to intervene?

We three educators have worked with many disenchanted and disengaged students. We have interviewed them, surveyed them, read the literature about them, and tried to make a difference in their academic lives. This book is a result of many years of experience and research, as well as many failures and successes. It is presented to the reader with a profound belief that each child can learn. We say "each" rather than "every," because learning and teaching involve individuals. Each individual is different and may need a different strategy to motivate him or her.

This book presents some reasons why youngsters might disengage themselves from the learning community along with ideas for reinvigorating their academic selves. We believe that adults in their lives can make a difference, regardless of the circumstances causing this self-destructive attitude. We don't have all the answers, but we have hope that our ideas will help spark encouragement for the educators, parents, and mentors who work with disenchanted and disengaged youths. Kids tell us individually that they want to do well, but they don't know how, are in situations that prevent them from doing well, or feel that the work they're expected to do is not worthwhile. Many have come to believe that no one *can* help them, that adults have given up, and that it just doesn't matter. We know better.

When they say, "Teach me—I dare you!" we accept the challenge!

1

Understanding Those Who Dare Us

Jesse was not looking forward to the new school year. Everything and everyone would be new, and that would be a challenge. Lack of success in elementary school had led to lack of success in middle school. Entering the high school would probably be no different.

Students who dare us to teach them are like the game of Jeopardy. They fall into several categories, require us to ask many questions, make us skeptical about their outcome, and reward us with their success when we do help them learn. As teachers, we cannot afford to let them lose.

Although there is no standard category for all who dare us to teach them, there is a profile that fits most of them.

- ◆ They generally are skeptics about life in general.
- ◆ They are not sure that what schools have to offer them matches their current or future needs.
- ◆ They disguise themselves well in the current dress of the day and fade into the culture of their age group.
- ◆ They ask and freely give advice to each other about solving their problems without the benefit of experience or adult consultation.
- ◆ They believe that they are indestructible and that whatever they will need in the future will be given to them with little or no work.
- ◆ They take life-threatening risks with alcohol and drugs.

- Some take the opposite position of defiance and antagonism.
- They define the counterculture in the school and hide within many disguises of themselves and what they fear they may become.
- They are both males and females.

Every school has a growing percentage of those who still come to school, still come to class, and still need more help than they are willing to ask for. They are the students who give you the look that every teacher recognizes, the look that says, "Teach me—I dare you."

Spend a morning in an eighth- or ninth-grade classroom, a classroom where students are involved with the teacher and each other. Watch the dynamics of the interaction, listen to the discussion, and try to determine who in that classroom is not achieving near their potential, is not keeping up with the rest of the class, and is not receiving the support they need to have a positive learning experience. Which of the students has, by middle school, developed an attitude that, if verbalized, would say, "I'm here; I need help; teach me—I dare you."

Although all students may fit this profile for a short time during their schooling experience, there is a growing number who are truly at risk for not finishing high school or even middle school. Because the outside influences on children and adolescents can change daily, early and accurate identification of these students and intervention by classroom teachers are essential to the students' survival in school.

Traditional definitions of students at risk include those who are potential dropouts; those who have failed one or more grades; those who demonstrate poor grades overall; those identified as special needs; and those who have high absentee, truancy, or tardiness rates. "At risk" has also been used to describe those who abuse drugs and alcohol and those who have a minimal identification with the school. Boys more than girls and students from low-income families are also defined as at risk. In a typical classroom, those characteristics can be embodied in one student or in several. Those who are identified are more apt to receive school help than those who fall within the group of students who are on the fringe of developing serious at-risk behavior unless someone intervenes.

There have always been children who were disenchanted and disenfranchised from the school system. There have always been struggling readers, truants, and those who have created discipline problems. What has changed is the number of students, the degree of risk, and the rapidity by which students become at risk. Good teachers can readily identify those students who are struggling academically, socially, and emotionally. Students with poor school adjustment are the topic of many faculty meetings, team meetings, and parent conferences. Consider the following classroom.

It's 10:15 a.m. in a typical school. Some of the students in this science class are being taught about the water cycle. Others are not. At the third table from the back, a girl is filing her nails while daydreaming of her adventures of the past weekend. Next to her, a boy is drawing pictures of animals in his notebook. At the back table, there are two empty seats and one girl taking sketchy notes. She tries frequently to catch the attention of a girl at a table in the front row. While the girl in the front row is listening to the teacher, the boys next to her are feigning attention while they play tic-tac-toe. A boy from another table shouts out a comment about the teacher's shoes. Most of the students laugh, but several seem quite annoyed at the interruption.

The teacher divides the class into work groups for the experiment on water quality to be done. Four of the groups find the instructions and get to work, one group asks for further directions, and one group sits on the desks and begins to discuss a recent school event. Two male members of this group say the assignment is dumb and they aren't going to do it. They sit and watch as the other group members start the experiment. They frequently offer disruptive comments to get the group off task. As the experiment progresses, a girl in this group spills the water sample on the floor. As the teacher approaches this group to help, the two boys tell him, "This assignment is dumb. This stuff isn't important. It sucks."

This science class is full of at-risk and potentially at-risk students. It could be almost any grade level. In every classroom today there are students who challenge teachers to make the students learn. They lack intrinsic motivation and usually bring a self-protective attitude with them. Sometimes this attitude is one of bravado. Sometimes it is one of antagonism. Other students ooze boredom from their bodies as they sit in class. Usually it is cover-up for some other issue going on in their lives. Most either refuse to participate or disrupt the class with their outbursts. Some are gifted, some are learning impaired. Some have considerable support from home, others have none. All are affected by the events of the world outside of the school, including their neighborhood, their community, and the media.

Some are developing a history of school problems, others do fine until their lives are disrupted by events over which they have little control. Some of the events that put students in jeopardy include the following:

- Change in friends or peer group members
- Change in living arrangements (moving from one area to another, changing custodial parents, homelessness)
- Change in health and nutritional habits (eating disorders, alcohol, drugs, diet)
- Change in family (divorce, remarriage of parent, death, birth of sibling)

- Change in role models (from parents to peers and pop culture)
- Change in academic success (teacher expectations, grades, homework)
- Parental expectations for school and family responsibilities (too high or too low)
- Participation in out-of-school activities (time management, eligibility)
- Change in school structure (elementary to middle to high school)

Students who feel good about themselves, have support from adults, and have friends who like school can address problems and participate in school with greater commitment and expectation for success. Students who are facing significant life changes require a teacher who has a strong, consistent, positive self-image and the ability to help students develop their own talents and goals. Students in our society today seem to be rich in information but poor in action. They have a difficult time making important decisions that affect their lives. They may expect school to give them answers, but too often the required content does not match what they need and want to learn. Although states have implemented content standards, what is missing for these students are the essential life skills of decision making, problem solving, time management, and essential life abilities such as safe behavior.

When students respond to the mismatch between the process of schooling and their life necessities, they are labeled at risk. Although many continue to come to school with their problems and their attitudes, other simply find ways to drop out. Those who come to school are still hoping that someone will teach them what they want to know. They have not lost hope for help; but they do not know how to ask the right questions. So they sit in that science class filing their nails, playing tic-tac-toe, shouting out comments, and wearing a countenance that says, "Teach me—I dare you."

Teachers at all grade levels can identify and meet the challenges of these students. Recognition that there are categories of risk is the first step in meeting the challenges that these students bring. Categories of risk are determined by the degree to which the behavior affects the student's ability to participate in the schooling process and function in other life tasks. As students approach adolescence, the consequences for the behaviors also affect the degree of risk to the student. There are many classifications for students at risk, but anyone who has taught middle school or high school will agree that the normal process of puberty brings risk to students who have no other reason to be at risk. Students may be a part of several categories at one time and have several levels of risk within a category.

Category I: Students in Transition:
Socially, Emotionally, Physically, Morally, Intellectually

The first category of risk for children and adolescents is normal transition from one phase of development to the next. As children mature, their physical, social, emotional, intellectual, and moral development are all affected by internal and external influences. With the earlier onset of puberty and exposure to a wider range of social ills at an earlier age, the levels of adult expectations for children and children's expectations for themselves have changed. Books like *All Grown Up and No Place to Go* (Elkind, 1984), *Children of Fast-Track Parents* (Brooks, 1989), *Fires in the Bathroom* (Cushman, 2003), and *A Tribe Apart* (Hersch, 1998) describe new attitudes in American society that create risk for children and adolescents simply because of the era into which they were born.

Sometimes the influences are those of heredity. Body type, rate of development, and illness all affect children's perceptions of themselves and their interactions with the schooling process (Giannetti & Sagarese, 1997). Children grow up today aspiring to look like either a superathlete or a supermodel while their bodies grow into those that are dictated by their genes. The reaction of others to how one looks also creates risk for students as they choose to assert themselves or not in the classroom and social structures of the school. As students enter middle school, their response to bodily transitions must be accompanied with factual information and understanding adults who can answer their questions and respect their concerns.

Other developmental transitions include moral, social, intellectual, and emotional ones. As children develop prior to the pubertal years, their physical, social, emotional, and intellectual development are normally in sync. Once the pubertal process begins, the physical development can get a jump start on the other processes. Young adolescents can grow four inches during their seventh-grade year but still be socially and emotionally immature. They can develop intellectually but still be physically immature. It is the lack of synchronization that creates problems for many students and puts them at transitional risk. As the social need to fit in grows stronger, those who don't fit in create coping skills that may affect their performance in the classroom.

How students respond to their own transitional development determines their degree of risk. Consider the increasingly common student:

Cathy's grossly overweight condition in the seventh grade made her the brunt of jokes and the recipient of many cruel comments. Her self-esteem had reached a dangerously low level. In response to the comments and jokes, she found comfort in food. She read constantly by herself and did not participate in class activities. She hated gym. She found it easier to stay at home than attend school. She did not participate in class for fear she would be made fun of.

Her parents encouraged her to try several fad diets, but none worked for her. Her teachers encouraged her to participate, but none were successful.

This young girl is an example of the physical risk that many students experience today. Obesity in young adolescence adds high risk to both boys and girls going through puberty. At a time when being accepted is essential to life, it is not only the health risk but also the emotional risk that is elevated for this age group.

Other examples of students at transitional risk include boys who are slow to mature physically, girls who mature earlier than their peers, students who are extremely shy, students who have received accolades from their peers as the class clown, and students who accept without question the values of their peers over the values of their families. Most students make childhood transitions without incident, but those who have compounding physical, emotional, social, or environmental attributes may increase their degree of risk. A thorough understanding of normal development for children and adolescents will help those who work with them identify those who show signs of risk because they significantly vary from those parameters.

Gender has a significant impact on how a student transitions from childhood to puberty. Researchers agree that in schools at all levels, more attention from the teacher goes to boys because they are louder and demand more attention. Boys tend to have better spatial abilities, such as measurement and geography, whereas girls tend to have more verbal skills. Boys have more difficulties with reading, which creates an increasing transitional risk as the complexity of the material increases. Boys display a range of attention-getting devices and are more physically aggressive (Gurian, 2001). Perhaps that is why teachers and principals were quick to name those male students they considered at risk, but had to thoughtfully consider those females in their classes and schools (Bergmann, 1989).

Current brain research also implies that the processing of planning, setting priorities, suppressing impulses, and examining consequences to decisions and behavior may not be finished until age 25. Therefore, the transitions brought on by the hormonal changes of puberty have a major impact on how students respond to instruction all the way through high school. Those same students may also take uninhibited risks with alcohol and drugs because of the abundance of dopamine in the brain in the late teen years (Wallis, 2004).

Because many of the transitional difficulties of middle and high school students are governed by their hormonal and brain development, there is an increasing need for adults who understand how this impacts learning.

Category II: Students at Risk from Their Environment

The second category of risk includes students who are affected by environmental influences that they cannot control. Both poverty and wealth can create risk for children. Family structure and attitude toward education, location of the school, community support of students, pressure for academic success, and parental involvement are all factors that have been researched and found to affect the success of students in school.

Local mores and culture are established by the students in their school. These often conflict with those held by the adults in that same environment. Students are quick to notice mixed messages and develop a "so what" attitude toward school. They are also astute observers of double standards imparted by teachers and administrators.

Being a part of a particular environment means that students develop social skills to participate in that environment. Consider the risk that students take to participate in the alcohol and drug scene in certain towns. Environmental risk runs the gamut from students lacking the necessities of life to students having so many material items that nothing has any value.

Environmental risk also involves the group interaction that takes place within the school. Students who bring heavy baggage to school from home have their chances of risk compounded. Even fourth graders can be unkind and not accepting of those who are different. The "you can't be in my group because you don't have the right clothes" dilemma begins for girls as early as third grade. This lack of peer acceptance leads girls to seek acceptance in socially unacceptable ways. Supervising an elementary school playground can be a lesson in why students are at risk in the classroom. Every school has its bullies and its victims.

Bullying causes one group of students to inflict their emotional, social, and physical damage on another group. Playground interactions soon spill over into classrooms and affect the performance of those who are victims as well as those who are perpetrators. Victims, in particular, tend to respond less often in class, participate in fewer activities, and refuse to confront their attackers. By the time these same students reach the sixth grade, many of them are at risk, both environmentally and socially.

Other actions within the school that create environmental risk include lack of support personnel to help students who are academically challenged, lack of guidance support, and lack of communication with parents. Identification of this category is done by reading cumulative files, speaking with teachers from previous years, observing students, and talking with students and parents.

Category III: Students Who Lack Social Skills

This category includes those students who lack the social skills to be accepted by others. The skills used in groups of children and adolescents for communicating with others, sharing ideas, working on projects, and taking part in activities are generally developed as children grow and interact within their family, their neighborhood, their church, and their school.

For students who are shy or abused at home or who are without adequate appropriate role models, the transition into the school becomes a nightmare. In the larger context of the classroom, their lack of social skills stands out. Take for example, the case study of the following sixth-grade student.

Today was one of those days when she just couldn't concentrate on long division. She had not done the homework because she was getting ready to move again. She wondered what her new school would be like. Would sixth graders there be nicer than the ones at her current school? She had only been there six months, and she had not made any real friends. The other students basically ignored her, but the teachers were nice. She was a member of a family that moved often to wherever they could find work. She desperately wanted to make some friends.

This young girl is just one of many students who are socially at risk in our schools. She did not choose to live this lifestyle, but she will soon drop out without appropriate intervention. She is a topic of meetings, in-service days, teacher concern, and election campaigns. She is a child left behind in the most literal sense of the word. She begs the question of how she and other children and adolescents like her survive and achieve in the inconsistencies of her life. She is rarely with a group long enough to make friends and practice her social skills.

Category IV: Puberty and Social Risk

While children and adolescents develop at different rates, they all grow through the same physical changes. Although puberty comes sooner now than it did in past generations, it is still a biological process that brings with it new appearance and functioning of the human body. Risk may be created when puberty brings with it accompanying expectations that the child will socially be able to do things that older students can do and have the logic to go with those actions.

Because everyone develops at their own rate, it makes it difficult for students who want desperately to fit in to look or feel different from their peers. Puberty can cause risk for students who have no other reason to be at risk when they feel like they do not fit in.

Category V: Students Who Are Academically at Risk

Students who lack foundational basic academic skills in reading, math, and writing become increasingly more at risk of failure as the level of content material and the level of expectations increase. Some develop complex coping skills and are passed from grade to grade by a thin margin. Some are passed because they do not cause any problems. Some are not recognized or identified until it is too late. Others attend remediation classes and programs and try to obtain the skills necessary to do the school work. They say, "Teach me—I dare you" in a different tone from those with social or environmental risk.

Academically at-risk students are easily identified by reading and math achievement tests or state test scores. Usually they are reading at least three grade levels below their peers. They may have other skills at which they are competent and therefore may not be identified early by their teachers. Although girls may be underachievers in this same category, boys usually outnumber girls six to one in remediation programs. The following case study is about a young man who illustrates the plight of these boys.

Joe sat in the bleachers watching his friends and classmates walk across the stage and receive their diplomas. He should have been with them, enjoying the accolades from parents and family, but instead he had failed his senior year in high school. He had always struggled with school, especially English and reading, but somehow he had managed to keep up until this year. As the expectations and the amount of work expanded, he fell further and further behind. It was hard to fake the reading when the material included more difficult novels, sophisticated vocabulary, and articles that held no meaning to his life. He had relied on his friends to help him out before this year, but they had either graduated and moved on, or had to focus on their own academic work in preparation for college. Not only did the reading hamper him in English class, but the concepts and reading in government class were more difficult to understand. He was afraid to approach a teacher for help, and turned to alcohol to ease the pain of his failure. Nothing in high school except football held any real meaning for him. His grades had been barely good enough to keep him eligible at the beginning of the season, but he was injured and the motivation to remain eligible was gone. His hopes for other athletic activities were diminished by the need for knee surgery. In his mind, there was nothing else he could do well except play football.

So he sat in the bleachers, wondering how he would complete the work for his government and English classes and finally get his diploma. He wanted to finish high school. He wanted to play football again. He wanted to be what he had hoped to become.

This student is an example of those students we see every day, students who we realize are struggling, yet we still pass on without adequate skills to keep up. He is one of the thousands of students who inspire good teachers and administrators to ask these questions:

- When do students become at risk?
- To what degree must they be at risk before remedial actions are taken?
- What support systems do at-risk students need?
- What characteristics do at-risk students display?
- Are the risks for girls different from the risks for boys?

If a student has not been identified as at risk until high school, chances are slim that he or she will be identified at all because of the lack of teaming and teacher communication. It will be a counselor or special education teacher who recognizes the degree of risk. A particular problem for this type of student is transition from one school to another. Records frequently arrive after a student has been placed in a class or set of classes that may or may not be appropriate. Many times these students come from another state or country and have no records.

Category VI: Gifted Students Who Are Not Challenged by the School Curriculum

Students at this level are those who are gifted and not identified or challenged in school. They may not know of their own gifts until some content sparks an interest. They may not have parents who understand giftedness and have low expectations. In many ways, they are as much at risk as those with academic reading difficulties. Consider John.

When John was in fourth grade, what he really wanted to do was have a long conversation with Tolkien about *The Lord of the Rings*. He wanted to know what had actually inspired Tolkien to write the trilogy. However, his assignment was to answer the questions at the end of the chapter, all of which required only recall and minimal comprehension. In eighth grade, John longed to discuss the status of the government in Afghanistan with his senator and wrote him several letters. He received confirmation that his letters were received, but no opportunities to offer his suggestions. In history class, all John was expected to do was to make a time line of World War II. He was not challenged. He completed the application for the national chess tournament and wrote an essay on Hawking's theory of the universe just for fun during chemistry class. He already knew the chemistry and had in fact written a letter to the editor of the class text to correct an error on one of the lab activities. Teachers saw John as disinterested and a potential troublemaker. His basic lack of social skills, coupled with his high level of intelligence, created confrontations with teachers and administrators on a regular basis.

Other students made fun of the comments John made in class. They never included him unless forced to do so in group work. They said his ideas were weird. They basically left him alone. He was alone most of the time when he was not in school. He decided that being included with his peers was more important than being smart and stopped doing any work in his classes.

Not all students at risk have academic achievement problems. Some have such serious social interaction problems that their lack of social skills eventually causes them to drop out or seek alternate and undesirable ways of being accepted. This case study depicts the dilemma for teachers faced with challenging the gifted kids who are as much at risk of not achieving as those who lack academic skills. Teachers frequently ask how to reach the gifted students in their schools so they do not become at risk. The question of social acceptance also brings a complex counterpart to the problems of academic risk.

These students are often picked on by other students or left alone. The lunchroom identification system works well with this type of student. Walk into the lunchroom someday and just look around. Locate the students who are eating alone. If this happens most days, they are probably at risk because they have ideas or habits that are not accepted by their peers. They are alone in the hallways and in all their classes. They do not participate in extracurricular activities.

Category VII: Students Identified by State Guidelines as At-Risk

Every school year, teachers get a list of those students who have been identified by state guidelines as at risk or in need of special services. They are usually categorized by a specific learning problem, disorganization, emotional/behavioral action, or physical limitation. Some are identified because of truancy, absenteeism, or court orders. Others receive special help from one or more specialists in the school. Others are wards of the court and have regular school visits from their probation officer.

Nationally, over 25% of all students fall into the category of at risk and drop out of high school prior to graduation. Most of these students do not care that higher standards and more frequent testing has been mandated by the No Child Left Behind program. They are the children left behind and are the victims of lack of early intervention. Many large school districts ask fourth- and fifth-grade teachers to identify those students whom they believe are at risk of dropping out of school. Frequently used criteria include poor grades overall (D average or lower), low reading scores, failure in an earlier grade, lack of participation in extracurricular activities, attendance in more than four schools, lack of acceptance by peers, frequent tardiness or absenteeism, truancy more than three times a semester, rebellion against authority, and poor handling of structured activities.

The range of special needs is very broad, and most are difficult to identify as the student gets older. Most classroom teachers have not been trained to identify or remediate special-needs students. Often they try remediation that is inappropriate for the need. One school district's only advice for teachers included the suggestion that they mark an asterisk by the names of students they thought might be at risk and keep an eye on them.

Few districts today have a long-range plan for helping students at risk or teachers who teach at-risk students. Often these students are very intelligent in most areas and have difficulty or a disability in just one area. Consider the case of Sam.

Sam could never do math. She tried all through elementary school and was taught in a variety of ways. She learned to fake it and could memorize words and times tables, but never knew what they meant. In sixth grade she was finally tested and found to have a serious learning disability in math. She had no number identification skills at all. For seven years she had been faking it or relying on friends to help her. On the other hand, she was an extremely gifted writer. A very astute English teacher in seventh grade recognized Sam's unusual talent for writing and encouraged her to use it by writing poetry. She published a book of poetry in eighth grade titled *Reach for the Moon* (Abeel & Murphy, 1994) that won many awards. Sam received special help in math in middle and high school, but today still lives with her disability. She has spent several summers as an adult talking with teachers about learning disabilities and gifts. Her message is simple: everyone has disabilities, and everyone has gifts. Your job is to find the gifts and get help for the problems.

Other students in this category may have organizational problems that keep them from achieving. They are easy to observe and require special help with just the skill of organization. Consider the following student.

Her books fell to the floor as she opened her bulging locker. Papers flew in several directions as Elena desperately tried to find her assignment book, her social studies homework, and her pencil. She grabbed what looked like her homework and ran to class. As the teacher began reviewing the homework, she realized she had grabbed an assignment from two weeks ago. It was already graded and marked down for being late. As she realized her error, she also was aware that the teacher was now giving directions for a new assignment that was due tomorrow. She leaned over to ask her friend what he had said and immediately got in trouble for talking. Without her notebook, which was still back in her locker, she had nothing to write on. Therefore, the assignment did not get written down and she forgot all about it as she went back to her locker to look for her math homework. And the process started all over again.

Category VIII: Special Education Students

Special education students have been identified in elementary school or are being tested in middle school for learning disabilities, emotional disorders, or social disorders. Some have physical disabilities or multiple special needs. Most have an Individualized Education Plan (IEP) that states their remediation and learning plan. Because they are already receiving services and have a wide range of difficulties, they may be a part of the "Teach me—I dare you" group, but they do have resources identified for them. Because most are included in regular classrooms and have special teachers to assist them, their category may be the easiest to assess and get resources for.

Category IX: High-Risk Students

High-risk students are those who may or may not come to school but are unattached to family, friends, and school. They seem to lack a conscience and suffer from antisocial personality disorder (Magid & McKelvey, 1989). They are psychopaths who run the gamut from mildly impaired to criminal. In their book, *High Risk: Children Without Conscience,* Magid and McKelvey (1989) propose that these children never bonded or became attached to their mothers or adult caregivers as infants. Other research indicates that these students may be abusing drugs and alcohol. They may play the game of school, but plan, while there, to cause harm to others. This level is rare in most classrooms, but needs recognition because of the antisocial acts committed by these students in school. The shooting at schools in the 1990s brought recognition to high-risk students and the need for early intervention with them.

Although many high-risk students drop out, others stay in school and affect the culture of the classroom and the school itself. Many teachers are heard to say, "I have one student who requires more attention than all the others put together. I give this student all the help I can, but the student doesn't seem to care"; "I think this student needs more help than the school can give"; "I am afraid to place this student near others; the student always tries to hurt someone." These comments are indicative of a teacher with a potential high-risk student. Often when a school recognizes that a student is high risk, the parents deny the possibility and the student cannot receive proper outside help.

High-risk behavior is frequently observed on the playground in early elementary school. One school described the early elementary behaviors of a sixth grader who had been charged with assault. This student would hit others all the time. Nothing except isolation seemed to help, and then when allowed to join the group again, this student would commit an even more serious assault on another student. The student would find rocks or sticks and throw them in the faces of others. All efforts to get parental cooperation had failed. The boy's parents said the school was being overreactive and refused to sign for outside intervention. They did not want their child labeled.

After two years of attempts to gain help for this student, the school involved the local police in the playground incidents and each assault received police attention. In eighth grade, the student used a floor hockey stick during a supervised gym class to purposefully and seriously injure two other students who just happened to be nearby. The student said he just felt like hurting someone that day. The school administration school finally got help when the parents of the injured students pressed charges against the high-risk student and the courts required placement in a juvenile detention center and psychological help for that student. The disruption and aura of danger created by that one student took more administrative time than all the other students put together in that school. Although the school followed all state guidelines in trying to obtain early intervention for that student, its hands were tied by lack of cooperation and denial from the parents.

Interviews with middle and high school students indicate that they all agree that there is at least one student of high risk in every school. With the number of school tragedies in recent years, attention has been drawn to this category of students, but the procedures for getting help take far too long. This level of risk usually involves students who have multiple problems that far exceed what the classroom teacher can and should be expected to address. Outside intervention and parental involvement are essential to helping this student.

All of these are examples of students at risk in our schools. Although many students in Categories I–VII have no serious medical problems or learning disabilities, they are failing and the system is failing them. Every one of these students can achieve and could probably do so with support, guidance, mentoring, and change of environment. They are true examples of students at risk who sit in our classrooms every day. They are analogous to the lemons of the automobile industry. They are rushed through the system with little attention, and they then cause serious problems for others and themselves. They require us to ask questions, provide services, and change our behaviors to deal with theirs. They require a systemic change in the way most schools look at students.

The Search Institute (www.search-institute.org) has identified 40 developmental assets that affect student success. By assessing students' attainment of these assets, a school may find ways to adjust the educational environment to optimize student success (Scales and Leffert, 1999)

Resources and References

Abeel, S., & Murphy, C. (1994). *Reach for the moon.* Duluth, MN: Pfeifer-Hamilton.

Bergmann, S. (1989). *Discipline and guidance: The thin line in the middle level school.* Reston, VA: NASSP.

Brooks, A. A. (1989). *Children of fast-track parents.* New York: Viking Penguin.

Cushman, K. (2003). *Fires in the bathroom: Advice for teachers from high school students.* New York: New Press.

Elkind, D. (1984). *All grown up and no place to go.* Reading, MA: Addison-Wesley.

Giannetti, C., & Sagarese, M. (1997). *The roller coaster years: Raising your child through the maddening yet magical middle school years.* New York: Broadway Books.

Gurian, M. (1996). *The wonder of boys.* New York: G. P. Putnam.

Gurian, M. (2002). *The wonder of girls: Understanding the hidden nature of our daughters.* New York: Atria Books.

Gurian, M., & Henley, P. (2002). *Boys and girls learn differently.* San Francisco: Jossey-Bass.

Hersch, P. (1998). *A tribe apart: A journey into the heart of American adolescence.* New York: Ballantine.

Magid, K., & McKelvey, C. (1989). *High risk: Children without conscience.* New York: Bantam Books.

Moir, A., & Jessel, D. (1990). *Brain sex.* New York: Dell.

National Middle School Association. (2003). *This we believe: Successful schools for young adolescents.* Westerville, OH: Author.

Scales, P., & Leffert, N. (1999). *Developmental assets: A systhesis of the scientific research on adolescent development.* Minneapolis: Search Institute.

Sollman, C., Emmons, B., & Paolini, J. (1994). *Through the cracks.* Worcester, MA: Davis.

Wallis, C. (2004, May 10). What makes teens tick. *Time Magazine*, pp. 56–65.

Websites on the Developmental Characteristics of Adolescents and Young Adolescents

www.nmsa.org/research/ressum5.htm
www.bloomington.in.us/~bbbs/adolescents.htm
www.children.smartlibrary.org/NewInterface/segment.cfm?segment=2435
www.search-institute.org

Websites on the Developmental Characteristics of Students at Risk

www.nwrel.org/scpd/sirs/1/topsyn1.html
www.nacada.ksu.edu/Clearinghouse/AdvisingIssues/FAQs/atrisk.htm

2

Identifying
Why the Dare Is Made

*Jesse entered the ninth-grade English class after the teacher had
given the assignments for the next week. Not wanting to disturb
the other students, nothing was said by either the teacher or Jesse.
The teacher was happy to note Jesse's presence after his two weeks
of absence.*

Recent studies have attempted to determine the scope of the problem of
at-risk students in the United States. In 2003, data supplied by the U.S. Department of Health and Human Services from their study on U.S. children
with emotional and behavioral difficulties indicated that 2.7 million children
between the ages of 4 and 17 had definite or severe difficulties in emotions,
concentration, behavior, or being able to get along with others as indicated by
their parent (Simpson, Bloom, Cohen, Blumberg, & Bourdon). They also
found that poverty was significantly related to whether or not children had
difficulties. White non-Hispanic and black non-Hispanic boys were more
likely to have had difficulties than Hispanic boys were. In 2003, 71.2% of children with difficulties that lasted one month or longer had difficulty with
learning. More than one third of the children who had difficulties that lasted
one month or longer had difficulty with leisure activities (Simpson et al.,
2003).

Many attempts have been made by federal agencies and state depart-
ments of education to find ways to classify and identify students and their

degree of risk. The bottom line in all studies is that it is the parents and the classroom teachers who are the first ones to notice students who are having learning and socioemotional difficulties.

Identification of students means asking the right questions to determine the category of risk for each student. Gathering data can be as basic as taking time to read cumulative folders, meeting with teachers who have had these students the year before, talking with counselors and social workers, conferencing with parents or guardians, and using test data to look for academic deficiencies.

Identification of students at risk usually includes only those who qualify for special education services, chronic truants, absentees, or those who have language problems. Although all of these students are certainly at risk, there is a larger group of at-risk students who slip quietly through the system with minimal attention to their plight until it is too late and they have dropped out physically, emotionally, and intellectually. Those students are the ones that still come to school, come to class, rarely participate in extracurricular activities, and gradually fall through the cracks because they don't have discipline problems.

Identification by Teacher Talk

Listening to teachers talk about students allows an informal system of identification. Comments heard at team meetings about the same students week after week should be perceived as a cry for help. If a team or group of teachers agrees that the same student is continually having or creating problems, then that student needs more help than the teachers can give. Teachers talk about those students who sleep or "drift off" in class. They talk about those who are chronic forgetters when it comes to assignments, directions, or materials. They talk about those who struggle with language or are overwhelmed with the structures of math or science. They talk about those who cannot write legibly. They talk about those who are discouraged or disagreeable. Listening to teacher talk is another way of identifying students at risk, but the people listening must be willing to take action and follow up with observation and discussion with the student and the teacher. Teachers, administrators, and counselors must talk together about these students. Team meetings in the middle-level schools have been the most effective means of allowing these conversations to take place. All parties that interact with the student can be present and provide information.

Identification by Asking the Essential Questions

There are essential questions surrounding this group of students that must be asked by those who teach and administer them. There are strategies that can be used to encourage and assist them. As the pool of dropout candidates grows, educators must ask the following questions:

- ◆ Which students in our schools are really at risk?
- ◆ What are the characteristics of a student who is at risk?
- ◆ Are there degrees of risk?
- ◆ Which kinds of at-risk behaviors can the school deal with?
- ◆ How can professionals and parents determine whether or not a student is at risk?
- ◆ Why are some students more at risk than others?
- ◆ What school and societal structures create risk for our students?
- ◆ How does teacher behavior affect at-risk students?
- ◆ What is the culture of our school?

Once the answers to these questions have been obtained, school personnel can then determine interventions for individuals and groups of students.

Identification by Observation of Students and Their Records

There are as many different categories and descriptors of students at risk as there are research studies that have been done. Perhaps a more simplistic starting place with identification is in the process of observation. Looking at students as individuals, looking at school records, and looking at how students interact in the classroom and the hallways are all places to begin. A common practice is for students to transition from the elementary school to middle school and middle school to high school with no one except the counselors really looking at their history or records. Too often, middle and high school teachers do not have access to more than reading scores, and few actually look at the ones that are available. Looking at student records is a good way to recognize potential risk in all students. Although some students transition into a new school already at risk, others become at risk while they are there. A classic teacher training film, *Cipher in the Snow,* (Brigham Young University, 1973) reminds teachers how easy it is to miss the signs of risk and abuse in children. In this film, a child in the school dies of neglect, and no one remembers anything about him. The film is a poignant example of the importance of simply knowing the names of one's students and understanding the baggage they bring to school.

Identification by Shadow Study

Another technique for observing students that are perceived to be at risk is to complete a shadow study of the student. This process requires an observer (preferably a teacher, administrator, or counselor) to spend an entire day with a student observing and recording what that student is doing and what the class is doing every three minutes. This process allows the observer to get a comprehensive look at a day in the life of an at-risk student.

While costly in time needed for the study, this process also allows the observer to see where the student may be achieving some success and what interventions are working. This information should be summarized and shared with all school personnel who interact with this student. The student should also be interviewed about his or her perceptions of the day at the end of the day with questions like these: What was the best part of your day? What was the worst part of your day? What did you learn today? When did you need help today? Such questions are good starting points. Samples of national studies using the shadow study format are available from the National Association of Secondary School Principals (see www.principals.org publications for examples).

Identification by Sharing Concerns About Students with Other Teachers

Simply changing a student's environment can put him or her at risk. After educators have looked at the students and their backgrounds, it helps if the school adopts a classification system of categories of risk and a strategic plan that provides support at each level. One middle school confronted their growing numbers of at-risk students by holding a faculty meeting the first week in October and asking each teacher to write down the names of five students they were concerned about. When grade-level lists were combined, the students at risk were identified with few surprises and much consensus. Teachers were then able to discuss alternative ways of helping each student. They started by having each teacher "adopt" two students for the year and become responsible for supporting those students.

Several high schools have implemented a seminar in their daily schedule as a time when students can connect with one teacher and see all teachers for help with their studies. Other schools have established committees to develop long-range plans for supporting students who show early signs of risk or who have been previously identified. All of these plans must consider the context of the environment in which the school is located. Too many times, the outside influences seem overwhelming to both the students and the school system itself. Schools must identify the elements over which they have little or no control in the lives of their students and determine what they can do within the context of the school without becoming overwhelmed with the other risks their students have. A middle school teacher in a school with an extremely high mobility rate in Florida once said, "Give me a student for six weeks straight and I'll work a miracle, but I cannot teach them if they aren't here."

Identification of School and Societal Structures That Foster At-Risk Behaviors

School and societal structures that foster at-risk behaviors range from family and neighborhood attitudes toward education to serious substance abuse. These are elements over which children have very little control and by which they are frequently victimized. Children are resilient, but they also need continuity, consistency, and hope to participate and achieve in school. A mile or a neighborhood block can make a gigantic difference in the risk that society heaps on children. Schools in areas where there is high incidence of family mobility have special needs in identifying students and determining whether or not they are at risk.

Hundreds of federal and state projects have been implemented to help level the playing field of education. Schools are located in neighborhoods and communities. The degree to which a community respects and appreciates its school is reflected in the amount of support that is given outside of the school to youth. Students only go to school six or seven hours a day. A community that supports its schools provides additional opportunities for activities and interaction outside of regular school hours. If a community provides nothing for its children, the school itself cannot keep students from being at risk.

All elements of the community's social structure, including juvenile court services, police liaisons, parent networks, youth organizations, church groups, Girl Scouts and Boy Scouts, and 4-H, must work with the school to identify and help those students who are at risk. Community governments must talk about how much they value the youth of their community and then budget for programs to support the schools.

If a community does not value its youth, there will be "no place for the kids to hang out and nothing for them to do." There will not be jobs for youth in the summer, and there will not be a group of people who agree with the old adage that "it takes an entire village to raise a child."

Schools' strategic planning for student support must include the community personnel who deal with students outside of school. The most successful committees that have seen real progress have included teachers, parents, students, health department personnel, police liaisons, representatives of various religious groups, and community planners. Student representation is essential to the committee's efforts, because students provide the reality check that is so often missing in educational decision making.

Students are quite capable of telling educators how schools can be improved and what issues of risk students are facing. Often, they provide insights that adults would never hear about. When in doubt, ask the students.

Misperceptions of Student Behaviors

Although most educators agree that any student can be at risk on any given day for a variety of reasons, there are stereotypes and misperceptions that must be communicated to teachers and students so that those students who truly need help will get it. Too often, teachers do not see passivity and lack of participation as potential risk. Girls mask their lack of involvement and achievement in school by using social skills to feign interest in classes.

In a study of 250 middle school students who were most frequently sent to the office as discipline problems, all of the students were identified by the principal as being "at risk," and none were currently placed in special education programs. Cumulative months of lost learning time was the outcome for this group (Bergmann, 1989). They all were "frequent offenders" of such rules as not talking in class, bringing one's gym clothes, and being on time. Because of the frequency of their infractions, they were simply sent to the office for punishment rather than being dealt with by the teacher. When their silence or absence said, "Teach me—I dare you," the teachers read that as disruption and sent them out.

Schools who do frequent student surveys have at least attempted to allow student input into the climate and culture of the school. They may have a better chance of accurate assessment of risk than those who use assumption as their guide.

Matching Identification of Students with Goals for Student Success

To include only present characteristics and levels of students in a school discussion would leave out a very important guiding question: What do we want our students to become, both in school and in life? Most schools would agree that their students need the following:

- To achieve both academically and socially
- To feel that they are needed and can make a contribution to the world
- To forecast and organize to meet the future
- To read all kinds of material with understanding
- To know how to access information and set priorities from that information
- To be compassionate and practice compassion
- To understand where they are in the world
- To develop tolerance for differences
- To be physically fit
- To be unconditionally loved by at least one other person (Lee Salk)
- To have organizational skills
- To recognize and use their talents
- To develop a sense of humor
- To learn civility and an appreciation for the arts, music, and environment

An inspection of school goals and mission statements usually includes most of those needs stated in a variety of ways. If schools combine the identification of levels of students with agreement of what they want their students to become, they are on the way to developing a system of communication that can only begin to benefit those students who are at risk.

Opening the dialogue is an essential step in the process of teaching the students whose faces say "Teach me—I dare you." Answers to the following essential questions can be obtained by administrators who gather faculty members, parents, community representatives, and students. Using the database of information gathered by this group, the school can then begin to develop a plan of action that will help teachers help these students. Essential questions for administrators, teachers, and parents include the following:

- What do we know about the young people in our school and our community?
- How do we know this information?
- How do we interact with the children and adolescents in our school and community?
- What is our local definition of students at risk?
- What is our plan for helping students at risk?
- How effective is our current plan?

- Are there new areas of risk to be considered in our community?
- Can we double-dare the students who dare us to teach them?

When schools have answers to the essential questions and have identified their at-risk population, they can they determine the degree of risk for each student, for girls, for boys, and for specific groups within the school. Teachers can be educated in the fine line between risk and normal development in children and adolescence. When the entire school system is using the same definitions and identification measures, then a plan for changing classrooms and the school to fit the needs of these students can be made.

Schools also recognize that there is outside baggage that students bring into the school with them that contains the factors of students' lives over which they have little or no control. Poverty, hunger, drug abuse, high mobility, disease, violence at home, parental education level, and necessary jobs are all elements of that baggage. Students who succeed in spite of those obstacles are usually in schools that have recognized those elements in their community and developed support systems for their students.

Resources and References

Bergmann, S. (1989). *Discipline and guidance: The thin line in the middle school.* Reston, VA: NASSP.

Brigham Young University, pub. (1973). *Cipher in the snow* [Motion picture]. United States: LDS Motion Picture Studio.(Available for review and purchase online at www.Idsvideo.com/CipherInTheSnow.htm)

Simpson, G. A., Bloom, B., Cohen, R. A., Blumberg, S., & Bourdon, K. H. *U.S. children with emotional and behavioral difficulties: Data from the 2001, 2002, and 2003 National Health Interview Surveys.*

Websites on Identification of Students at Risk

www.cdc.gov/nchs
www.penpages.psu.edu/penpages_reference/28507/285072900.HTML
www.dropoutprevention.org/stats/whos_risk/sit_risk.htm?source=arise
www.education-world.com/counseling/personal/at_risk.shtml
www.bhsu.edu/eduation/edfaculty/cpollard/websites.htm
http://education.indiana.edu/cas/adol/adol.html
www.ericdigests.org/2000-3/early.htm

http://education.qld.gov.au/health-safety/promotion/drug-educa-
tion/html/m_risk.html

www.motivaton-tools.com/youth/at-risk_who_succeed.htm

www.nacada.ksu.edu/Clearinghouse/AdvisingIssues/FAQs/atrisk

3

Motivating
Those Who Dare Us

Jesse wondered what might make the school day and the world seem more meaningful. There were so many things to think about and so little connection between the curriculum and Jesse's life. Jesse was sure there were more students who felt the same way, but he didn't do anything about it.

Charlie sits in his English class with a faraway look in his eyes. He has come to class, once again, without his book or a writing utensil. He doesn't cause any outward behavioral problems, but he doesn't do any work, either. His biggest accomplishment for the entire class period is taking the pass to go to the restroom.

Melinda sits in the same class writing feverishly all period long. Unfortunately, this class is supposed to be discussing the reading assignment given the previous day. Melinda never volunteers an answer and seems put off when her teacher calls on her. Melinda's typical response is a shrug of the shoulders.

What is happening with these kids? Do they lack motivation? Or is the problem that they are motivated, but not about the work they should be doing for school?

Few people are *un*motivated—*something* drives us all to action. Charlie may be motivated about fixing up his car after school and may spend time in class thinking about it. Melinda fancies herself as a Dear Abby, spending her time writing and answering notes with her friends. So although these students may seem unmotivated in the class we're teaching, they are indeed motivated. The question becomes, how can we capture their attention enough to turn them into successful learners?

Motivation can be defined as a quality that initiates and sustains behavior. It can be intrinsic or extrinsic. Intrinsic motivation drives a person to participate, to set and strive for goals, to reflect on progress, and to take pleasure in accomplishment. It is learning for learning's sake. It fosters perseverance and initiative, even in light of setbacks and obstacles. Extrinsic motivation spurs a person to action because of some outside influence, like working for a good grade, pleasing parents, or sidestepping a negative consequence. Both kinds of motivation can direct a person's behavior, but intrinsic motivation is self-induced and can be sustained for longer periods of time.

Most of our disengaged students are impervious to extrinsic rewards or consequences. They no longer respond to threats or cajoling. They don't care if they disappoint their teachers or their parents. They act only if the goal is chosen by them or is of relevance or importance to them. It is apparent, then, that to engage these hard-to-reach students, we must abandon efforts of reward and punishment and strive instead to help them build intrinsic motivation, or, at the very least, determine goals that they will want to reach.

Pause for a moment and think about your own motivation. What factors influence your motivation? Are you either motivated or not, or is there a continuum of motivation? If you start on a task, then give up, does that mean that you lost whatever motivation you had?

Compare your list of motivational factors to those listed here:

- Interest in the task or subject
- Perception of the task as fun, pleasurable, or fulfilling
- Feeling that the task relieves stress
- Relevance or importance of the task or subject to one's own perceived needs
- Immediate usefulness of the skill or information
- Avoidance of negative consequences
- Desire for positive consequences
- Confidence in one's ability for success in the task
- Respect for the context of the situation or the person directing it
- Self-satisfaction in work well done or a challenge met
- Perceived necessity of the task in light of one's circumstances, including group conformity.

We can sort this list into three categories: those that involve the task itself, those that depend on the context in which the task is being presented, and those that refer to self-perceptions. Braddock and McPartland (1993) categorized motivational influences as classroom tasks that are interesting and relevant to one's future goals, a caring and supportive environment, and opportunities for success at challenging tasks. We'll look at each of these factors individually, although some examples will certainly overlap.

The Task

Let's admit it—people are all different. Some like working on cars; others settle for remembering which side the gas tank is on. Some enjoy spending a snowy afternoon curled up with a good book; others would rather strap on snowshoes and head for the woods. When a family goes shopping, one person may happily spend time in the hardware store, another in the bookstore. But even a person who finds hardware stores boring will head there if snow shovels go on sale the day before a blizzard. Even a high-energy athlete might stop in at the bookstore to pick up a gift for a favorite aunt. People's shopping habits differ because their interests differ—but where they shop can also be influenced by their needs, their wants, or even a catchy ad campaign. By the same token, teachers can set out to increase student interest in the things to be learned.

Much of the research on motivation is indicative of the **expectancy value** theory. Expectancy value theory suggests that "people orient themselves to the world according to their expectations (beliefs) and evaluations" (retrieved January 13, 2005, from www.tcw.utwente.nl/theorieenoverzicht/ Theory%20clusters/Public%20Relations%2C%20Advertising%2C%20Marketing%20and%20Consumer%20Behavior/Expectancy_Value_Theory.doc/ index.html). This theory assumes that the intensity of motivation is determined by the learner's expectations for success and by the incentive value of the goal. If either of these two components is missing, then no effort will be invested in a learning activity. On the other hand, if students are provided with the value of a learning activity and if a reasonable effort is applied, students can be successful at completing learning tasks.

Let's think about tasks in the school setting. Even the most disengaged students are *sometimes* interested in *some* subject matter. What we know is that in order for students to be motivated, their tasks must be interesting, relevant, and challenging but within their reach. Other students may start to work on a task but lose interest quickly and stop working. So we must deal with at least two types of disengaged students—those who seem to lack interest or motivation and those who lack perseverance. We'll address both.

Let's revisit Charlie, the disinterested student in English class. Amanda Turner had this young man in class. When she discovered that Charlie was fixing up an old Camaro, she brought in *Car and Driver Magazine* and other resources that she thought might capture Charlie's attention. It worked. Charlie did research, wrote papers and even composed some poetry about cars (and one memorable poem about his teacher). Mrs. Turner had discovered Charlie's interest and used it to spark and maintain his motivation.

A 16-year-old seventh-grade student in a science class showed little interest for anything academic. But his teacher discovered that he loved to draw and hired him to create bulletin boards and draw science illustrations on handouts and tests. This student used his study hall and lunchtimes to work on his drawings in the science classroom. His teacher explained to him what needed to be illustrated, creating a comfortable conversation about the subject matter. He did the drawings, signed them with a flourish, and learned some of the content. He legitimately earned a C grade in the class; the classroom handouts got terrific artwork; and the trusting relationship that developed between student and teacher had multiple benefits for both.

Sometimes the relevance of our subject matter is unclear. Sometimes it doesn't exist. If students don't find relevance in a task, they tend not to give it any attention. How many social studies teachers struggle to teach latitude and longitude? How many students can even remember which is which, never mind mastering the concept of imaginary lines circling the earth, with measurements in degrees, minutes, and seconds? But in Alaska's coastal villages, students grasp the details at an early age. Their families own fishing boats and use latitude and longitude as navigational tools. They understand the relevance and use of this intricate system. They apply the concept in their real lives.

Perseverance, then, can often be related to the task itself. It's easier to give up on a concept or project if it's not interesting or important. It's easier to continue working at a task when its value is evident. But we need to know that we stand a chance of success.

It should come as no surprise that remedial and "low ability" classes have a preponderance of disengaged and disinterested students. Frankly, they are bored. They describe their work as repetitive and "stupid" ("it sucks"). They realize that the standards and expectations are low-level and therefore of questionable value. Who can get excited about tasks they have seen repeatedly and consider to be inane? There is no thrill in mastering low-level tasks, so why bother? Many of our students have never felt the rush of conquering a challenging and important task. Therefore, they look for the rush elsewhere. "There's always going to be a low-level class," said one eighth grader, "and I'm always going to be in it."

If nobody offers hope or seems to have confidence in a student's skills and abilities, why should the student make any effort? We all need to be involved in what we perceive as meaningful work. In too many classrooms, students work on tedious or trivial tasks day after day. An eighth-grade social studies class silently colors maps four days in a row. What's the point? An 11th-grade group sits through a 45-minute PowerPoint presentation on the architecture of New York City—and the only person who talks or moves is the teacher. Why pay attention? A sixth-grade class is asked to describe the process of mummification—a cool idea, maybe, but what is its real-life application? In a seventh-grade life science class, students spend their entire time copying down notes from the chalkboard—as the old joke goes, "the notes of the teacher transferred into the notes of the students without going through the minds of either." As educators, we can affect our students' motivation by the decisions we make regarding what we teach and how we teach it.

Implications for Educators

◆ Study the curriculum and make some changes. We must understand what it is that we want our students to know and be able to do. It is no longer satisfactory to depend on textbooks to decide what content we should be demanding our students learn. As professionals, educators must assume this difficult task. We should be able to articulate to students *why* they are learning a particular concept, and students must be able to see its relevance to their lives. Yes, we all now have standards that are assessed, but let's admit that much of what we are teaching is neither required by state or federal mandate nor necessary for student success. If we must grade students' learning, let's resolve to grade them on their progress toward learning important content, what Wiggins and McTighe (1999) call "enduring understandings." If someone asked each teacher at your school to pick a favorite test or exam, then merged the questions into one test and had all the teachers take it, how many would pass? Perhaps we ask too many trivial questions about trivial matters.

◆ Learn about individual students' interests, experiences, abilities, and achievements. Students' talents and individual expertise can be nurtured through attention to their strengths and accomplishments. Often we can tailor individual assignments to take advantage of students' interests, as Mrs. Turner did with Charlie. Charlie was still expected to meet all the objectives for the English class, but his reading and writing could be centered on cars, a topic he enjoyed.

◆ Challenge the students with new information and skills that are connected to prior knowledge. Help students set realistic goals. Scaffold their instruction carefully, giving precise feedback and expectations for success. Modeling learning outcomes can be a powerful instructional tool, and using "think alouds" helps students concretely hear the process. Students need to know exactly what is expected of them and how to go about achieving their goals. Show students examples of quality work. Assemble a portfolio of "best work" that students can look through to help gauge their own efforts. A student who doesn't know how to start an assignment may not do it at all—and may not bother to tell anyone why. Therefore, monitor each individual's progress; intervene early and often to keep potentially disengaged students on target.

◆ Use information about students' developmental characteristics and needs to design instruction. Students should be actively engaged in their own learning; they should be moving, sharing their ideas, reflecting, and self-evaluating. Students should be given learning choices so they can exert their growing sense of need for control. Remember that adolescents' attention spans are less than 15 minutes; they *need* to talk, and they *need* to move around. If the teacher doesn't plan for these actions, the students will drift off task to meet these needs. It's much easier to keep them going on the right path than it is to refocus them.

◆ Emphasize tasks over performance. Except for high achievers, young adolescents are more motivated toward specific tasks than individual performances (such as tests). Students tend to be more motivated when a clear learning goal is established rather than a mere performance goal. In other words, disengaged students are not likely to become motivated to learn material "because it will be on the test." They need a more personal reason to exert the effort, to master the task for its own sake. That's why authentic assessments are so much more valuable than traditional paper-and-pencil tests. Authentic assessments encourage students to perform real-life tasks rather than show off their knowledge and abilities for one person only—the teacher. A disengaged youngster with a disdain for authority figures probably won't work hard just for the teacher's approval or applause.

The Context

Many disengaged students defy us because they defy authority in general. Indeed, most young adolescents begin to question authority ("Whadda we have to do this for, anyway?"). They question adults as part of their quest to discover what is important to them. In addition, young adolescents typically seek excitement and activity. Often, the relationship between teacher and student and the climate of the school and classroom can make the difference between defiance and engagement.

Many disinterested students describe having a sense that their teachers don't really care whether the students are successful. MacIver and Plank (1996) state that "one of the most potent sources of motivation is to have caring teachers and peers who are rooting for them to do well, who are encouraging them to give their best in the classroom, and who are doing everything in their power to help them improve their skills and increase their understanding" (p. 1). Let's examine these characteristics in terms of the environment we maintain with our students.

A student teacher, Molly Gale, realized that her high school students were somewhat unenthused about her unit on the executive branch of the United States government, so she decided to exude exhilaration in the topic. She kept saying, "I just *love* studying the executive branch," and she designed lessons and activities that showed why. She made her classes exciting and emotionally charged and worked hard to build relevance into the content. She used her sense of humor and enthusiasm to create a motivating and energetic classroom environment. Most of her students responded. Some of her students began leaving her notes saying that they, too, *loved* studying the executive branch!

At a parent conference in mid-November, the mother of a disengaged sixth-grader described her struggle to get him up in the morning for school. Fred hated school; it was boring. Two weeks later, his team of teachers started a series of multidisciplinary units that incorporated lots of choices, authentic activities, various instructional strategies and student groupings, and challenging problem solving. The teachers, as coaches, met frequently with individuals and small groups of students to check their progress and reset learning goals. Fred came to life. He no longer had to sit still and listen. He became engaged in his learning and supported by his teachers and peers. At the April parent conferences, Fred's mom reported that Fred liked school so well, he wouldn't stay home—even when he was sick!

Likewise, recall the 16-year-old student whose teacher took advantage of his talent for art to hook him into a seventh-grade life science class. Once his academic environment reflected that his skills and abilities were valued, he began to respond. His defiant attitude gradually changed to a supportive presence. He became a positive voice in the classroom, encouraging other students to "listen up." He actually made up his mind to be the first in his family to finish high school.

Implications for Educators

- Students must perceive the environment as supportive and caring (see Chapter 4). Find out how your students feel by interviewing them, giving surveys, and having class discussions. The mere process of asking them for their opinions will facilitate students' faith that someone cares.

- Strong relationships between students and teachers are essential. Supportive adults other than parents are important to a student's healthy development (see, for example, Scales & Leffert, 1999). Students are more likely to work hard for someone they respect and trust. Teachers who base their classroom management on authoritarian practices and fear may have a quieter classroom, but not one where meaningful learning takes place. Learning is a risky human endeavor. Learning means questioning one's prior knowledge and conceptions and opening oneself to new and challenging ideas. A physically and emotionally safe environment allows such introspection to occur.

- To build a supportive environment, look for concrete ways to demonstrate the value of each individual in the learning community. Have students and educators share responsibility for classroom management. Class and team meetings can be helpful.

- Use humor, energy, and emotions to foster motivation, recall, and perseverance.

- Language and literacy are the cornerstones of effective teaching, especially for at-risk young adolescents. Strive for meaningful conversation among students and between students and the teacher. This discourse is an opportunity for the teacher to scaffold students to complex thinking and meaningful use of the language.

- Keep your classroom environment positive and optimistic. Personalize learning.

Self-Perceptions

How many of us are good at every sport we try? How many of us enjoy the ones we're not good at? How many people stay on the sidelines of the volleyball game at the company picnic, rather than be embarrassed by missing shot after shot? How many have taken a few skiing lessons and never gone back because falling down all day long just wasn't worth it?

Think about the number of "Teach me—I dare you!" students who never even try. People don't *want* to fail, but if they think that success is not an option, why try? Many of our students have learned over the years that they *will* fail, regardless of any effort they may expend. We have to change their minds about this perception.

Bandura's (1986) research on **self-efficacy,** a perceived sense of competence, presents a powerful argument for helping students see that they are capable of performing specific tasks. Many youngsters who don't try to succeed in school just don't believe that they can. They perceive difficult tasks as threats rather than challenges that can be overcome through effort. Therefore, these kids will work to avoid tasks and will show low levels of commitment and aspiration. Many of our disengaged students doubt their academic abilities. As the Efficacy Institute maintains, we need to legitimately convince students that they have the wherewithal to succeed academically. The institute's spokespeople have stated, "Smart is not something that you just are, smart is something that you can get." According to this theory, students benefit from setting attainable, challenging, short-term goals; receiving specific feedback on their progress; reflecting on their work; and seeing the task successfully modeled.

Can students improve their self-perceptions about their academic capabilities? Absolutely. Here are some methods to consider:

- ◆ Students must experience success. All people need to tackle challenges and master them. The key here is that the tasks cannot be easy ones with quick solutions. Students need to be supported through the process of working through challenging and meaningful work.

- ◆ Teachers and mentors must clearly demonstrate that they have faith in youngsters. Too often we send the message that we believe some of our students are "slow" or incapable of producing quality work. We often praise for the slightest product rather than for increasing amounts of effort. Students who are building positive beliefs about their capabilities must perceive that their teachers and mentors have faith in their abilities to succeed. We need to analyze the messages we send to youth.

- Students must observe successful social models. It is important for youngsters to observe people *who are like themselves* being successful. The "star" of the classroom is too far removed to inspire their emulation. Socially, students gravitate toward those most like themselves. They must see that individuals within that social set are able to succeed at school.

- Specific feedback is critical. Think about the feedback we give to kids' attempts at writing. Does it help to scribble "awkward" or "needs clarity" in the margin? Such feedback itself needs clarity. What specifically does the student need to work on to improve the writing? Can the teacher point out examples of good writing and help reword awkward writing? Can we set up specific writing goals?

Look, too, at Ryan and Deci's (2000) research on **self-determination.** These researchers argue that students *must* be included in their own goal setting. Students' sense of self will motivate them to do better on exams when they are perceived as a way to monitor their own progress rather than a way to determine a grade. Too often, we want to do something *to* at-risk kids rather that something *with* them. Self-determination theory assumes that we will not be successful unless we integrally involve the student in his or her own learning—in goals, strategies, and assessments. The student needs to be actively involved in all phases of learning to build intrinsic motivation.

Likewise, Covington's theory of **self-worth** explains that among a person's highest priorities is protecting one's feeling of competence. These theories may shed light on why so many students refuse to try: "If I don't try, I can't fail." Additionally, **self-handicapping** behaviors are ways students may circle their wagons to protect their feelings of competence. Some self-handicapping behaviors include procrastination, consciously putting forth too little effort, complaining often of fatigue or illness, and using illegal substances (see, for example, Riggs, 1992; Urdan and Midgley, 2001). What we realize is that many of our most challenging students are purposely avoiding the task to preserve their sense of self. Either they try (and fail) or they don't try at all and avoid the failure. We need to provide them with another option.

Many of our at-risk adolescents fail to perform well on achievement tests not because they lack the ability, but rather because they give up on the tasks or lack opportunities and experiences that higher achievers have had. Many of them don't even *try* to do well. They joke about filling in the op-scan circles with their #2 pencil to make a funny pattern. One student designed a picture of a fish—gills and all. He didn't read one of the questions on the test.

How do you eat an elephant? One bite at a time. Many disengaged students lack good time and project management skills; many have difficulty reading the text (for tips for helping reluctant readers, please see Chapter 4). These skills can be taught and modeled, allowing students to tackle smaller chunks of a task, get feedback allowing them to see concrete evidence of their progress, and find small successes along the way. Students need to learn that it is not their ability that stops them from conquering challenging tasks, but rather their approach to the problem or their limited experience with the steps necessary to perform the task.

Scholars such as McIntire (1996) and Sternberg (1999) call for the development of expertise in our youth—each of them. They argue that academic abilities can be learned through specific strategies and experiences that scaffold students to mastery. Every student should become an expert in at least one area in school. They need a reason to come to school and they need to feel that their area of expertise is of value.

Cooperative groupings are a sound teaching strategy, but not when some kids are always tutors and others are always on the receiving end of help. The 16-year-old science student who helped with the drawings for handouts got a head start on learning the terms. He could then help the other students get them right. For the first time in his long years at school, he helped someone else academically—and it made a difference.

Here's another thought to ponder. Researchers (see, for example, Dweck, 1999; Ryan and Deci, 2000) caution about the use of praise as a reward for performance. It's the effort that needs to be reinforced. Think about some of the bribes we offer youngsters to encourage them to perform a certain task or behavior. Can this kind of reinforcement build intrinsic motivation? Will it result in effective long-term learning habits? Or does it merely get us through an unappealing task? Think about this from a youngster's point of view: If the task is so unappealing that kids need to be bribed to do it, how much value can it have? And why should I do it for a toy or a slice of pizza? These kinds of rewards usually work for the kids who would have done the task anyway.

It's even worse when the supposed incentive is a prize awarded only to top finishers. The students whose efforts repeatedly fall short eventually lose interest. If they can't compete with the other kids in the class, why bother trying?

If you asked a group of struggling students whose help they would seek if they didn't understand a concept, some might name a parent. Many more might simply shrug their shoulders or mutter. Why do they hesitate to ask the teacher for help? Perhaps they get the impression that the teacher doesn't have time for them—that the teacher's attention goes to kids who "matter."

Implications for Educators

- By the time children reach young adolescence, they have long-established beliefs about themselves and their limitations. Rather than accept this status quo, educators and mentors must actually become change agents of their students' self-perceptions. Motivation *can* be learned!

- As long as we have low groups, we will have low-performing students to fill them.

- We cannot afford to equate low achievement with low ability. Slowing down the pace, using low-level materials, and addressing low-level objectives does not motivate students. Challenging them with relevant and meaningful content and showing them concretely how to be successful does. The level of challenge must also be within their reach. A batter can hit a baseball even if it's thrown high, but if it's really out of reach, no amount of effort will make a difference. That's why prior assessments are so important. Find out where each student stands in relation to the objectives you will be teaching. Then pave the way for differentiated learning. You can do micro-groupings to remediate kids who need it or extend the learning for kids who already have some experience in the content.

- Compare students' work to their own level of progress rather than to the work of others. Success should be defined in terms of one's own learning, not someone else's. Again, prior assessments make it possible to concretely judge how far a student has come. Portfolios are particularly helpful in this task. You can see (and so can the students and their parents) the progress they have made.

- Compliment students for their persistence and efforts rather than rewarding them for a good grade or praising them for their intelligence. They need to think of intelligence as a learned ability, rather than an innate characteristic they can't change (see for example, Dweck, 1999, and Sternberg, 1999). Teaching learning and study skills and helping students self-monitor their progress will help them to understand that academic setbacks can be overcome.

- Rewards often detract from a task, making it seem so unsavory that no one would attempt it unless bribed to do so. Extrinsic rewards may be used to hook a child at first, but intrinsic motivation has longer-lasting positive effects.

- Teenagers need to feel a sense of self-direction and autonomy as they strive to become increasingly independent. Student choice fosters motivation.

- Avoid using labels like "slow" or "lazy." Remember that students will live up to (or down to) the level of expectation set for them. Disparaging statements ("I teach in the animal house" or "These kids have mush for brains") bring down the teacher as well as the student. Instead of voicing the negative, we should be voicing the positive! Remember the self-handicapping and self-efficacy theories: Many of the students' negative behaviors are simply a self-protection device.
- Give students the chance to tell you or show you what they know. How many times are students disappointed with their grades on a test because they "studied the wrong thing" or "didn't understand the questions"? You might add the following directions to each assessment: "Tell me something you know about the subject matter that I didn't ask you." You'll be surprised at how much they *do* know!

Reflection Questions

How does your curriculum content reflect students' characteristics, interests, and needs? Are you teaching for enduring understandings?

Are the curriculum tasks required of students relevant, meaningful, or interesting? Do students know the value of learning the curriculum content, other than repeating it for a test?

Is the required content challenging but within reach for each student? How do you differentiate instruction to address student needs?

Do you model learning? Are the students certain of what good work should look like in each required task?

Do your students know how to study and read your subject matter? Do you help them understand the text and resources you are using?

Do you know how students perceive your classroom climate? Do they think of you as equally demanding and warm and responsive? Is there a mechanism for students to ask questions without drawing attention to themselves?

Are students given choice and options in the curriculum and assessment? Are students taught and encouraged to set personal goals and to self-evaluate?

Is the pace of instruction adequate so that students have time to reflect on their learning?

What do you do to help disengaged students find an area of expertise and academic success? How do you intervene individually with students who seem to lack motivation?

Resources and References

Bandura, A. (1986). *Social foundations of thought and action: A social cognitive theory.* Englewood Cliffs, NJ: Prentice-Hall.

Braddock, J. H., II, & McPartland, J. M. (1993). Education of early adolescents. In L. Darling-Hammond (Ed.), *Review of research in education, 19,* 135–170.

Covington, M. V. (1992). *Making the grade: A self-worth perspective on motivation and school reform.* New York: Cambridge University Press.

Dweck, C. (Spring 1999). Caution—Praise can be dangerous. *American Educator,* 4–9.

Efficacy Institute, Inc., Waltham, MA. www.efficacy.org

Lewis, A. C. (1995). *Believing in ourselves: Progress and struggle in urban middle school reform.* New York: The Edna McConnell Clark Foundation.

McIntire, J. A. (October 31, 1996). *Identity development in early adolescents: Seeking and nurturing expertise in each student.* Presentation at the National Middle School Association Annual Conference, Baltimore.

MacIver, D. J., & Plank, S. B. (September 1996). Creating a motivational climate conducive to talent development middle schools. *Report No. 4: The Talent Development Middle School.* Baltimore: CRESPAR, Johns Hopkins University.

Pajares, F., & Schunk, D. H. (2001). Self-beliefs and school success: Self-efficacy, self-concept, and school achievement. In R. Riding & S. Rayner (Eds.), *Self-perception* (pp. 239–266). London: Ablex.

Riggs, J. M. (1992). Self-handicapping and achievement. In A. K. Bogiano & T. S. Pittman (Eds.), *Achievement and motivation: A social developmental perspective.* Cambridge, U.K.: Cambridge University Press.

Ryan, R., & Deci, E. L. (2000). Self-determination theory and the facilitation of intrinsic motivation, social development, and well-being. *American Psychologist, 55*(1), 68–78.

Scales, P. (1996). *Boxed in and bored: How middle schools continue to fail young adolescents—And what good middle schools might do right.* Minneapolis, MN: Search Institute.

Scales, P., & Leffert, N. (1999). *Developmental assets: A synthesis of the scientific research on adolescent development.* Minneapolis, MN: Search Institute.

Sternberg, R. (Spring 1999). Ability and expertise: It's time to replace the current model of intelligence. *American Educator,* 10–13, 50–51.

Urdan, T., & Midgley, C. (2001). Academic self-handicapping: What we know, what more there is to learn. *Educational Psychology Review, 13,* 115–138.

Wiggins, G., & McTighe, J. (1999). *Understanding by design.* Alexandria, VA: ASCD.

Websites:

www.apa.org—Type in "motivation" in the search window. Enjoy lots of interesting articles and research.

www.efficacy.org—Everything you want to know about self-efficacy. This information is invaluable.

www.ericdigests.org—The ERIC clearinghouse has several excellent articles about motivation and teaching at-risk kids. There are also several articles about the risks of rewards.

www.ldonline.org—Ideas for differentiating instruction and presenting content in various ways.

www.learningpt.org—Learning Point Associates, North Central Regional Educational Laboratory. Strategies and research on school improvement.

www.mcrel.org—Mid-continent Research for Education and Learning. Lots of good resources for teaching kids at risk and content area reading.

www.nmsa.org—The best source for reading material about young adolescents.

www.search-institute.org—Wonderful resource for information on developmental assets and supporting kids.

4

Connecting with Those Who Dare Us

Jesse studied the notice on the school bulletin board: "Those students who are interested in taking guitar lessons should sign up in the band room." Guitar was a major interest of Jesse's, but the teacher might be like all the rest.

School personnel can create a caring and supportive environment for at-risk students by involving students in the process of designing that environment. Because the adult perspective is often different from that of an adolescent, especially when it comes to the peer group, it becomes necessary to educate the adults in the building about the components of that perspective and how it affects the learning process. To make the information specific to the culture of a specific school, either a survey or interviews must be done with students. Surveys and interviews should be designed to answer the following questions:

- ◆ Who attends your school? (The answer to this question is found in demographic and attendance data.)
- ◆ What do they believe in?
- ◆ What do they think is important (priorities)?
- ◆ What are their future goals?
- ◆ What experiences have they had?
- ◆ What do they expect from school?

- ◆ What are their strengths?
- ◆ What do they need help with?

Data gathered from these surveys can be used by the faculty and administration to design specific programs and policies that affect the environment and culture of the school. Further data should be gathered from the faculty, asking them the same questions about their students. This enables faculty to test their perceptions of their students and compare them to the actual student data.

In addition, faculty members should each be asked to list the names of five students about whom they have concerns. These lists should go to the administrator, who can compile the lists and search for repeated names. Teachers who have done this have often been surprised at some of the names that appeared on the list.

The next step is to determine the level of risk for each of the students on the list and determine what interventions should and can take place. The following case study illustrates the outcome of one such study.

The first-year teacher was quite nervous when called to the principal's office during the week before school was to start. The principal had called her in to inform her that he had been analyzing reading data, and her fourth-period class of 10th-grade English would be a unique group of young men.

They were all excellent football players, he noted, but they had all had serious problems in ninth-grade English. It would be her job to "keep them eligible for the football season" and hopefully teach them something about English. She was welcome to use whatever materials necessary to help them succeed. That conversation in no way prepared her for the poor academic self-image held by these boys. Most were convinced that they should drop out and join the army or just drop out and go to work. They all had the "Teach me—I dare you" slouch and stare.

It was the football coach and the promise of a good season that had lured them back to school at the beginning of their 16th year. A quick perusal of their grades and test scores revealed that most had passed ninth grade with a D or D- in English, social sciences, and science. Some had done better in math. All were reading at least four grade levels below the 10th grade.

Serendipity intervened for this first-year teacher as she ate lunch one day at the same table with the driver education teacher. He was not looking forward to having this group of boys in class, even though they were motivated to get their driver's licenses. Realizing that reading the manual might be a major problem for the boys in her fourth-period class, she asked if she might obtain extra copies of the manual to use in her class. The driver education teacher gladly agreed.

With the lure of the license on her side, she convinced the boys that improving their reading skills was a worthy goal. She did not start with the manual, but started by giving the boys an opportunity to be accepted by a group of students for the ability they did have.

She connected them with the school in a unique way and gave them the dignity that comes from helping others. With a quick trip to the nearby elementary school she had procured several teachers who could use reading assistants in their classes. Starting with one-on-ones in the kindergarten, the boys of fourth period soon were reading children's books to the kindergarten students on a weekly basis.

Gradually they moved through the elementary grades as readers and tutors for small children. Their status as football players made them heroes in the eyes of the younger boys, and their confidence in their reading improved as they read to the children. As they moved to the middle school as tutors, they began to ask for more and more help with their own reading skills. When they learned the basic reading skills that they had missed, they practiced reading the manual for the driver education class. It was a winning situation for all of the boys—on the field, in the classroom, and in the community.

As the boys completed 10th-grade English with average or above-average grades and procured their driver's licenses, the new teacher reflected on a process that had used a variety of strategies for success. The key elements in motivating these students had included acceptance of the students as learners; connections to other students; recognition of their abilities; effective communication within the schools; and maintenance of their dignity.

Connecting Students to the School

There are several pragmatic ways to foster a feeling of acceptance in students. First, students must feel that they are accepted in the school and in each classroom in some way. Someone must know who they are and that they are there to learn. The following case study portrays a school where these students feel comfortable.

It did not matter to the principal if a student lived in an unstable home with a low income and parents who were not high school graduates. It did not matter if they spoke English as a second language, had a negative self-concept, and wanted to be somewhere else other than school. What mattered was that they showed up to school in the morning and stayed for the entire day. It mattered so much that every day he stood in the doorway of the middle school for all the years he was the principal and personally greeted every student with a smile, a handshake, and a positive comment. Students stood in line to get their greeting, and for many of them it was the most positive moment of their day.

This principal believed that the outside lives of many of his students could encourage them to leave school as early as the eighth grade, and he was determined to keep them all there and have them learn as much as they could. His determination was contagious among his faculty, and they too created an environment that supported all students. There were comfortable reasonable guidelines in the building for behavior and respect. Students understood that expectations at this school were different from they were in the neighborhood or at home.

If they needed help they knew where to go and how to get it. The tone set by the principal in that building created an environment that allowed adults to build effective relationships with all the young adolescents who attended that school.

Students feel connected to schools that want them to be there, involve them in the learning process, and offer them numerous ways to expand their talents. They connect with teachers who know enough about them to understand their developmental needs, appreciate and differentiate for their individual learning styles, and listen to them.

Sometimes school is the safest place for students to be, and they feel connected because they feel safe. Some students feel connected to adults in the building who are not teachers but support personnel who listen and understand them.

Schools that have developed advocacy programs have helped many students connect to a teacher who might not otherwise have done so. The original purpose of advocacy and advisory programs was to provide every student in the building with an adult who knew them, knew them well, and helped them negotiate the process of schooling. In addition, students who have mentors, tutors, and weekly meetings with counselors also feel more connected to the school.

Connecting Students to Other Learners

Students of the "Teach me—I dare you" group have tenuous levels of connection with the school, their peer group, the curriculum, and extracurricular activities. One of the most frequently asked questions by these students is, "So what's the point?" They follow that question with commentary about their lack of potential and resources to help themselves. Students who feel that they can better their lives by attending and participating in school can be taught, even if they dare the teacher to do so.

Students feel accepted when they fit in with their peers. They feel empowered when someone recognizes their talents or gives them the opportunity to succeed on their own. Self-acceptance and peer acceptance come when students can master the curriculum requirements on their own or feel comfortable asking for help. There are many factors that work against connections in school. Those factors are found in their out-of-school lives.

An essential step in connecting students to other learners is identifying what they can and cannot control in their out-of-school lives. Many times, the control found in a school is the antithesis to what a student encounters at home. Disruptive students who lack social skills often become the victims of a discipline system that says, "Don't do that," but does not tell or show students how to behave appropriately. As one sixth-grade girl told her teacher, "Everyone tells me to mind my manners, but nobody tells me what manners are." To teach the at-risk student is to model for them what is appropriate behavior in a variety of social settings.

Students who are willing to come to school are willing to learn social survival skills, even though their countenance may imply that they are not. Students who are comfortable with their own social skills are more apt to participate in class and school activities.

Shyness, as well as cultural and language differences, may contribute to a student's level of risk. Teachers and administrators must complete an analysis of the invitational nature of their own school prior to planning programs for at-risk students. There are several guiding questions that a planning group might ask:

- How do we know this is a school for students? Is their work displayed and changed often?
- Who welcomes people to our school? Are they trained in the art of civility?
- How do students make the school their own?
- How are informational signs written in the school?
- What are the school rules? How are they worded? Are there so many that they disconnect students?
- Where do our students live?
- What do the parents expect from this school for their child?
- What is the cultural makeup of our school?
- How many languages are represented in our school?
- How do students communicate with each other?

Most schools have discussed and written school improvement plans that include provisions for dealing with students at risk. Most of those committees did not include students and therefore missed the most important data.

Many schools have formed discipline committees to think of every possible infraction that a student can commit and then have tried to write rules to match those infractions. They expect their students to misbehave and write their rules accordingly.

Others try to write a few guidelines that all people can understand and live by. For example, a high school that had over 100 rules also had a corresponding number of discipline infractions on a weekly basis. Some students decided to see how many of the rules they could break. A new administrator decided that their rules were creating more risk for students than any other element of the school. She gathered a committee of teachers, students, and parents to create a new discipline system for the school. They agreed on three basic concepts which became the guidelines for the school community:

- Respect others, their property, and their right to participate in classes and school events.
- Be on time.
- If it is illegal on the outside of school, it is illegal on the inside.

Those guidelines were accepted by the students, and most of the discipline problems stopped. The guidelines helped put the emphasis back on learning. Those students who are on the verge of being at risk for attendance, behavior, and attitude could comply with a few good rules. They didn't feel compelled to "try to beat the system."

Connections come when students are involved in the creation and maintenance of the system of schooling. Their voice should be heard at all levels of decision making. In addition to the need for a caring attitude in school are the necessities of a comprehensive system of communication with the families of all students, a climate of expectation for achievement, frequent progress reports, a strong system of communication among teachers, and a mission statement that outlines the fundamental objectives of the school and the resources necessary to meet them.

One of the most effective ways to connect students who dare you to teach them is to place them in a group with accepting, competent students. Those groups may have an academic, athletic, or extracurricular emphasis. Allowing at-risk students to suggest extracurricular activities can lead to unexpected leadership and success on their part. In the classroom, letting students choose their own groups often ends with all the at-risk students in one group. This often leads to lack of progress. Pair shares, peer tutoring, topical triads, and group homework assignments are several positive ways to connect students to each other in the classroom.

When in Doubt, Ask the Students!

A simple way to connect students to each other and the school is to ask them how they feel about the school and how they feel they can be more connected. Teachers can ask all students how to connect them to the classroom, the material, and the school. The best ideas come from the students themselves. This process should always be done in writing so that even those who are afraid to speak in class will be willing to contribute. Many teachers keep a set of note cards in their classroom and pass them out periodically for student input on a variety of topics. Some teachers keep a question box in their room so that students can ask questions about issues related to the content or the school. Frequent questions from questions boxes over the past 10 years have included the following:

- Why is my family so messed up?
- Will I ever fit in?
- What do I need to do to be smart?
- Who can I ask for help with my homework?
- What can I do to make my mom listen?

There appears to be an almost desperate cry from students at risk for someone to listen to them.

Extracurricular Activities

At-risk students tend not to be involved in traditional extracurricular activities because of cost, discipline or attendance problems, or lack of encouragement. Sometimes the school does not offer activities that interest the at-risk student. Some students exhibit behaviors that cause problems with their peers, particularly in a team situation. Family problems, drug and alcohol problems, work schedules, and lack of eligibility from grades or credits keep others from participating.

As they fall behind academically and have no positive extracurricular experience, students can become more and more problematic for the school and their self-esteem falls. Therefore, the school needs to seek input from all students as to what kinds of activities should be offered. Schools can make connections with the community to cosponsor after-school activities and even summer programs.

Several schools in Michigan have recently assisted small groups of students (many who were at risk) by facilitating their work with the city council to get a skate park built. Students who had never handed in homework or participated in classes became articulate and enthusiastic presenters at the city council meeting. They were highly motivated, and the school used that motivation to connect with them and connect them with each other in a positive way.

Connecting Families to the School

Students feel accepted when their families are connected to the school. A higher level of parent involvement in the school causes higher achievement levels in students. Early research on students at risk indicates that many are identifiable by the third grade, with the numbers increasing with the age of the students. Reading ability, parental involvement, attendance, and family mobility are all early indicators of risk potential. Parent and family attendance at school events, both social and academic, is an easily observable indicator to teachers of students who may be or become at risk.

For years schools bemoaned the fact that at parent conferences the parents of the students they really needed to see did not attend. When they switched to a model of student involvement in student-led conferences, the attendance of parents increased dramatically. Most parents or guardians, if they are physically able, will attend a function at school in which their child is participating. Music presentations, plays, athletic events, and classroom projects are often more welcoming and less threatening to parents than is a conference with the teacher. When the student leads the conference, the threat is gone and both parents and child can feel that the conference is a positive, not negative, situation.

Student-led conferences are just one of several ways in which the school can empower the students and involve the family in a positive manner. Other means of support include advocacy programs, family nights at the school, home visits by teachers and administrators, accurate information about the composition of the student's family, a variety of ways for parents to be involved, and frequent parental and teacher discussion with students about their school experience.

Often the parents of students at risk have had a negative school experience themselves and mistrust efforts made by teachers. It starts in the early grades, when the majority of the news from the school about a student is bad. If teachers only communicate when the student is doing poorly, parents learn to expect bad news. Their supportive role at home becomes antagonistic as they conclude that the school is the source of the family problems.

In recent sessions at the National Middle School Association conference, the Secondary School Principal's convention, the Elementary School Principal's convention and several Parent Teacher Organization workshops, participants were asked to list the most effective process used in their school to involve parents as partners in the learning process. Their compiled lists included the following successful activities:

- Open houses, family nights, and parent nights, where families are introduced to teachers, programs, facilities, and curriculum.
- Homework hotlines and parent hotlines, where accurate and up-to-date information is available about assignments and events.
- An adult advocate in the school who has regular contact with the parents.
- Support groups for parents who have specific needs (single parents, language difficulties, location, and time).
- Parent education workshops on how to help your student and when and where to ask for help.
- Agendas for students that are signed by parents, flyers or refrigerator magnets with phone numbers of people to contact in school.
- Good news notes and phone calls.
- Student-led conferences.
- Conferences at times when working parents can attend.
- Cultural appreciation assemblies and days planned and implemented by parents.
- Communication of the curriculum expectations in an easy-to-read pamphlet for each grade level. This pamphlet includes topics, approximate months of coverage, and specific projects that need to be done at home or may need extra time.
- The development of a parent network for the monitoring of social events held in homes. Parents who agree not to serve or allow alcohol or drugs and to chaperone said events sign up and share the list.

In the home, students must have resources, time, and a place in which to do their work. Transportation to the public library or from after-school study programs is also essential to the support of students at risk.

Teaming is the Key!

When teachers are in teams, the process of family communication and support becomes much easier to implement. Consider the following case.

One seventh-grade team in a large urban middle school was concerned about the lack of progress of one third of their students. Many were falling behind, not handing in homework, and frequently absent on Fridays.

During the team meeting they talked about what assignments were usually given and what the expectations were for each of their classes. They invited the other teachers who had their seventh graders to the team meeting for a brainstorming session. Because it appeared that the problems were occurring on Fridays, it seemed essential to find out what the students did on Thursdays. Some speculated that there were sports activities or out-of-school events that were keeping the students from doing their work.

The team divided the students during the next day's advocacy session and asked all students to write the answers to the following questions:

- What is the best day of the week in school for you? Why?
- What is the worst day of the week in school for you? Why?
- What would be the best way to help you do well in school?
- What are some things you would really like to learn?

All of the students on that seventh-grade team completed the questions. When the team read the answers, they were astonished to learn that over one third of their students went to visit their noncustodial or shared custodial parent on Thursdays. That meant that the homework often did not go with them or they were out doing fun things with their parent, and they thought that Friday was their worst day because everything was due and they could not get it done.

The teachers discovered that they frequently completed units on Friday and that Thursdays were their heaviest assignment days. When they realized the social culture that was affecting their team, they switched their teaching calendars so that units were introduced on Fridays and little outside work was expected on that day. The achievement levels of the students went up because they could complete their work, and those students who were developing risk behaviors because they were caught in the middle got back on track.

Creating a Caring and Supportive Environment by Connecting with High-Risk Students

If the students who are at risk are chronic truants or behavior problems, they probably have been placed in separate programs that have tried to relate work to education, are small, and had low teacher-student ratios and extensive support services. Some have been placed in alternative schools where the entire focus is on the success of these students. Even within those programs there are students who bring the "Teach me—I dare you" attitude. Although every effort has been made by teachers in those schools to flex the curriculum, provide alternate means to receive credit and promotion, and tailor the lessons to the learning styles of the students, the most effective means of confronting the attitude is to connect with the student on a one-on-one basis.

One school had an at-risk student who only came to the classes during the day that one particular teacher was teaching. The rest of the time he was truant, but he never missed his science class. The student had an avid interest in race cars, and the science teacher used cars and racing as the motivator in the first lessons on motion and speed. The student came to science everyday because he connected with both the teacher and the content.

Other tough connections involve those students who are frequently in and out of treatment centers and homes for alcohol and drugs. They bring a challenge to the teacher to maintain the continuity of learning for the student. This challenge requires the teacher to make connections with the counselors, the parents, and the outside agencies if necessary.

Recognition of Student Abilities

Another essential element is the student's ability to participate in their own learning program. Too often, at-risk students feel that school is done to them with little opportunity to use their voices in the learning process. Giving students the ability to learn means giving them the skills and confidence to create their own destiny. Too often, the missing competencies of the "Teach me—I dare you" group are reading comprehension and multiplication of numbers. Students who feel that they cannot do the work often respond by fight or flight to save face among their peers.

There are at least four ways to connect students to their own learning when they are starting to disconnect from the classroom or the school:

1. Accurate assessment of reading skills and deficiencies.
2. Choice of reading materials that are essential to students and allow them to improve their reading skills.
3. Weekly self-assessment of progress toward classroom material.
4. Student choice of methods for showing that they understand the material.

Lack of adequate information about a student's reading or writing ability hampers teachers who attempt to help the student at risk. Reliance on standardized test scores for reading difficulties and general ability is not sufficient for analysis of the degree to which these students have problems.

Connecting students to their own learning means giving them assessments that describe specific skills that they must master before moving on to more complex material. If a middle or high school student cannot understand how to decode, encode, or put words together to make sentences that make sense, all the literature reading done in schools will serve only to frustrate this student more. Reading assessments that identify specific skills are necessary to truly help this student catch up. The emphasis in middle and high school should be on acquisition and mastery of those basic reading skills prior to involvement with multiple textbooks that are more difficult.

Expository texts, which are most often found in the content areas, are more factual than the basal readers of elementary school; have fewer pictures; have more tables, graphs, and diagrams; and are overwhelming to the below–grade level reader. In addition, fewer and fewer teachers in middle and high school have any training in helping students with reading difficulties. If a student falls behind and is disconnected from the material, a reading analysis should be the first step in assisting that student. The majority of middle and high school students with reading difficulties are young men. Interviews of at-risk students included comments by students that the material was either too difficult or totally irrelevant to their lives.

To motivate them to improve their reading means allowing for student choice in reading material and providing material that is essential to their survival. The high school teacher with a significant number of below–grade level readers in her English class who chose the state manual for driver's education for her English class also chose scripts from soap operas as reading material for girls who were staying home from school, watching television, and were below grade level in reading. Both attendance and attitude improved for these girls when the material was motivating. The goal for this teacher and these students was to connect to these students through reading material and improve their reading skills.

Self-Assessment as a Learning Tool

Connecting students to their own learning also means having them do regular self-assessment of their own progress. A weekly self-assessment instrument in each class helps students to monitor their work and determine where they need to spend their time (see sample in Appendix). In the fast-paced world of adolescence today, there is too little time given in class to reflect on progress or lack of progress, and students are surprised when they have fallen far behind in their work. This leads to either giving up or developing inappropriate coping skills.

Students who participate in the selection of projects and alternative ways to show that they have learned the material stay connected to the content of the class. When a teacher understands and implements the concept of multiple intelligences in the classroom, then multiple ways are available for students to learn and show that they understand.

Designing Successful Communication Systems

When teachers, parents, the administration, and students are all communicating effectively, the student is less likely to fall into the at-risk category. Too often, the failure to identify an at-risk student is the result of a breakdown in communication. There are eight steps to successful school communication.

Step 1: List current communication systems.

The first step in designing successful communication systems is to list the current communication systems in the school. Most lists will include the following:

- Teacher to teacher/team to team.
- Student to student.
- Teacher to student/student to teacher.
- Administration to teachers/teachers to administration.
- Administration to parents/parents to administration.
- Administration to students/students to administration.
- Teachers to parents/parents to teachers.
- Student to parent/parent to student.
- School to community/community to school.

While there may be other systems in place, the most important task is to determine how effective the communication is within the listed groups.

"Teach me—I dare you" is a challenge to a communication system. It may be a challenge to an individual teacher, a team, the principal, or the entire school. It can also be a challenge to a parent or the community. The levels of risk discussed in Chapter 1 can give some indication of how schools may confront the communication breakdowns that lead to at-risk behaviors in students.

Step 2: Give teachers, counselors, and teams time to share information about students.

Effective teams talk about all of their students, not just the ones who are having serious problems. Teams become frustrated because they talk about the same students all the time and make little progress. Usually those students have been talked about for years and need more help than the classroom teachers can give. Talking about all students on a team with a checklist of outcomes allows those students who may be at the initial stages of risk to be recognized (see Figure 4.1). When teachers share their perceptions of student progress, they may learn that one or two students have fallen significantly behind in the past six weeks or that several students are doing better. Once they share the information about all students, they can determine the level of risk for the student and develop strategies to help. Frequently, this discussion by teams leads to a request for reading information about those students. Most likely the students who are developing the "Teach me—I dare you" attitude have poor reading scores and are developing ineffective coping skills. Teams may also need information from parents about the students. When teachers meet to talk about students, fewer students fall through the cracks, but when teachers make a concerted effort to talk about *all* of their students, risks are diminished before they escalate into major learning problems.

Figure 4.1. Checklist of Students on a Team

List all students on the team.

Name	Needs Recognition	Needs Resources	Needs Referral
Student 1			
Student 2			
Student 3			
Student 4			

Step 3: Construct a visual diagram that shows all personnel and resources available for getting help for a student within the school.

List who in the school handles reading, discipline, attendance, language, socioemotional, and physical concerns. In addition, list the steps to be taken in seeking specific help for a student.

There are so many new teachers and new students in every building that it may take weeks or even months to get help for a student unless teachers and parents know whom to call. Parents who are concerned about their adolescents may be reluctant to call the school unless they have a particular name or office to call. Too often, the "Teach me—I dare you" kids get sent as discipline problems to the office, where discipline is administered by secretaries or assistants. When teachers understand the problems these students may be having, they can then refer to the guidance office, the parents, the principal, or specialists within the building.

Step 4: Offer training for teachers in handling special needs of students in the classroom.

Most schools have special education teachers or specialists in behavior issues. Many districts have reading specialists. All of those teachers should be asked to share teaching and reading strategies with the other teachers in the building. Simple strategies like test design, classroom seating, nonescalation, and reading in the content fields should be taught to all teachers in the building. Sharing their most effective strategy is a valuable way to start a faculty discussion about teaching students at risk. Some principals have the faculty read a book about specific strategies together and then brainstorm how to implement the suggestions in the book. Several districts have trained a team of teachers in dealing with at-risk students and then charged those teachers with training their colleagues. Other schools have invited a panel of students to talk to teachers and parents about how to reach them and help them learn. Whatever model is chosen, information should be shared.

Step 5: Establish a connections program where every student in the building has one adult who knows them, knows them well, and cares for them.

In the middle school this is often called advocacy or advisory. Some schools just call it connections. In the high school it is often called seminar or advisory. Whatever it is called, the purpose is to connect with every student in the building on a regular basis. Time should be built into the schedule for the connections to take place. Gather information from parents about the students who will see each adult. One middle school designed an instrument that asked parents to do the following:

- Identify their adolescent's areas of strength.
- Identify any areas of concern about the school year or specific subjects.
- Describe their adolescent's learning patterns regarding organizational skills, homework, etc.
- Explain, historically, what type of instruction has been most effective in helping their adolescent to learn.
- Describe their adolescent's hobbies, interests, and skills that may not be evident in the classroom.
- Give any other information that would help the teacher to know the student better.

The information from this instrument was shared with each advisor so they could make a more effective connection with the student.

Step 6: Implement one-on-ones as a strategy for all teachers and students.

A frequently used strategy in connections programs is a process called "one-on-ones." This process simply means that the teacher has a one-on-one conference with each of his or her advisees at least once during a grading period. In this conference, the student shares how they are doing in their classes and how they are doing in school in general. This conference is usually held during the time set aside in the schedule for connections, advisory, seminar, or homeroom. Some schools shorten their schedule and make a connections period every two weeks so one-on-ones can take place.

Usually the teacher gives the students guiding questions to prepare for the conference. Some of those questions might include the following:

- What is the best thing that has happened to you in your classes so far?
- What are you learning in your classes?
- What are your goals for the next two weeks?
- Are there any school issues that I can help you with?

The teacher sits at the back of the room so that all students are in view and places a chair for the student facing the teacher, but not the class. Each conference should be no more than two minutes to enable the teacher to touch base with each student. They do not need to all be done on the same day. When a student who has been daring the teacher to teach them participates in a conference, the teacher can then arrange for a further appointment with that student. If students refuse to talk to the teacher, they can be asked to put their concerns in writing. The key is to open lines of communication so the teacher understands the reason for the dare and can refer the student for further help if necessary.

Step 7: Collect and distribute a comprehensive list of places and people in your community who work with children and adolescents.

This resource list will include organizations and individuals who have programs, places, and assistance for youth. Start with churches, the police department, the health department, local doctors, and community service groups. Many schools have found a wealth of assistance by contacting their local senior citizens group and asking for volunteers to help with reading and math. Ask volunteers to place textbooks on tape for those students who have reading difficulties. That way the student can read along with the tape and understand the flow of the material rather than struggling with the material.

Step 8: Help students learn the process of goal setting.

Students who are struggling for any reason need help focusing on the future. The process of goal setting can be implemented in the classroom or the entire school. Students should set two goals each week: one academic goal and one personal goal. Because most students are not used to this process, it will take some realistic examples to get them started. A realistic goal in one class may be to complete all the homework on time for one week. In another class, it may simply be to ask the teacher for help one day after school. A process of goal setting should include the following elements:

- A strength analysis for each student. "I am good at…"
- The areas of needed improvement. "I can improve by…"
- Goals set from both strengths and areas of improvement.
- Goals written down and placed in a realistic time frame (daily, weekly, monthly, etc.).
- Modeling of goal setting by the teacher and other adults.
- Recognizing outcomes of goal setting in the media.
- Celebration when students have met their goals.
- Having students list who and what can help them attain their goals.

Maintaining the Dignity of Students

Dignity is an essential element for teaching the students who dare you to teach them. A wise principal from a middle school in Ohio required all of the teams to make at least two positive phone calls home to each of their students every semester. In that school, teachers quickly learned to look for the positive things that students did and give those actions the dignity of a response. Parents learned to expect that news from the school would be something to look forward to rather than something to be feared. Good news about their child offered them family dignity.

The community was apprised of the good works of the middle school students via place mats made for service club luncheons. The place mats, made of paper and designed by the students, offered positive statistics for the community to ponder.

Statistics included on the place mats included:

- 96% of our students made significant progress in reading this term.
- 98% of our students were not given a referral to the office for discipline this term.

- 99% of our parents attended the parent conferences held during this term.

- 94% of our students are involved in extracurricular activities.

The local news media learned to gather the positive statistics from the school because that was all that was ever given out, and the community perception of the school was one of a dignified, successful, learning environment. One goal of the school was to offer a dignified learning environment where all students could be recognized for their efforts and accomplishments. The learning process and the recognition of all students became the primary culture of this school. Fewer and fewer students developed the "Teach me—I dare you" attitude because the expectation was that they would learn and be successful.

Dignity is described by at-risk students as "not being hassled when you don't know something," getting help without someone making a "big deal" out of it, and "being good at something no one else is good at." One astute young woman defined dignity as something she had never known. Others said dignity was when someone knew who you were. (Bergmann, 2005.)

Some schools have worked to expand their recognition programs in the school so that more talents and students may be recognized. Although some have given an effort grade, others have provided incentives to students whose grades have gone up in one subject per marking period and not gone down in any others. These incentives have ranged from special certificates, to notes home, to recognition on a special achievement listing similar to the honor roll.

When the elements of acceptance; recognition of ability; connections to school, family, and others; and dignity are present in the lives of young people, it is much more difficult for them to develop the "Teach me—I dare you" attitude. Those elements are interrelated and cannot usually survive on their own when the student is at a high level of risk. Recognition of the special needs of the at-risk student by the leadership in the school is the first step in developing a caring and supportive environment for students at risk. The second step is to formulate a schoolwide committee to design the community of caring and support.

Reflective questions for a school committee to investigate include the following:

- How accepted do students feel in our school?

- What specific things do we do to connect students to the school, the classroom, and each other?

- What do we do to connect families to our school?

- How do students assess their own work?

- How do we communicate with our parents and community to enhance the dignity of our students?

- How do we know what skills our students need to work on in reading and math?

- What methods, programs, and people are in place to help students make continuous progress in their basic skills?

- What ways do we connect the various levels of our schools?

- How do we know how our at-risk students feel about themselves, the school, their own abilities, their acceptance, and their connections?

- What materials and personnel do we need to provide connections for students at risk?

Although connecting the "Teach me—I dare you" student to the school is an effective technique for those students who are temporarily at risk, successful programs at the high school level have separated higher-level risk students from other students; given them small class sizes; related school to work; provided counseling and other support personnel; offered remediation programs, tutoring, child care, and substance abuse programs; and shown flexibility in tailoring the curriculum to the learning styles and needs of the students.

That decision should be made by a committee of teachers and administrators who have accurately developed a profile of their at-risk students and determined what interventions and learning environments are most suited for their needs. Most of the "Teach me—I dare you" students who are attending school and without serious social problems will remain in the regular classroom and require an adult in the building who monitors their total progress.

Resources and References

Allington, R. I. (2001). *What really matters for struggling readers: Designing research-based programs.* New York: Longman.

Bergmann, S. (2005). *Interviews with middle and high school students.*

Bergmann, S. (1989). *Discipline and guidance: The thin line in the middle level school.* Reston, VA: NASSP.

James, M., & Spradling, N. (2001). *From advisory to advocacy: Meeting every student's needs.* Westerville, OH: NMSA.

Kinney, P., Munroe, M. B., & Sessions, P. (2000). *A school-wide approach to student-led conferences: A practitioner's guide.* Westerville, OH: NMSA.

Klese, E. J., & D'Onofrio, J. A. (1994). *Student activities for students at risk.* Reston, VA: NASSP.

Lustig, K. (1996). *Portfolio assessment: A handbook for middle level teachers.* Columbus, OH: NMSA.

Marzano, R. J. (with Marzano, J. S., & Pickering, D. J.). (2003). *Classroom management that works.* Alexandria, VA: ASCD.

Purkey, W., & Strahan, D. (2002). *Inviting positive classroom discipline.* Westerville, OH: NMSA.

Search Institute, The. (1997). *The asset approach: Giving kids what they need to succeed* [Booklet]. Minneapolis, MN: Author.

Sollman, C., Emmons, B., & Paolini, J. (1994). *Through the cracks.* Worcester, MA: Davis Publications.

Other Resources

National Middle School Association. *Classroom Connections* [Quarterly publication].

National Parent Teacher Association. 330 N. Wabash Ave., Suite 2100, Chicago, IL 60611-3690. E-mail: infor@pta.org

Websites: Creating a School Culture

www.turningpts.org/tpcreating.htm
www.sagepub.com/book.aspx?pid=10102
www.nwrel.org/scpd/sirs/1/snap2.html
www.schoolculture.net/indicate.html
www.voicesforchildren.ca/report-Dec2003-1.htm

Websites: Creating a Positive Learning Environment for At-Risk Students.

www.dontlaugh.org—
www.e-lead.org/library/resources.asp?ResourceID=25
www.ncrel.org/sdrs/areas/issues/students/atrisk/at700.htm
http://pcentral.org/climate/disciplinelinks.html
www.ualberta.ca/~jpdasddc/incl/c63.htm
www.susd/org/district/currrinstruction/newteacehr/positiveenvironment.html
www.fsdb. k12.fl.us/rmc/training/inservice/environment.html
www.nmsa.org
www.nwrel.org/scpd/sirs/1/topsyn1.html
www.ed.gov/pubs/EdReformStudies/EdReforms/chap2c.html

www.klkntv.com/Global/story.asp?S=374106
www.bookmagazine.com/issue14/teenreads.shtml
www.ncrel.org/sdrs/areas/issues/students/atrisk/at5def.htm
http://ischolarship.bc.edu/dissertations/AA13043402/
www.search-institute.org

5

Minimizing the Dare: Teaching for Success

Jesse knew that if he could just design or build something in class, he could show his teachers how smart he really was.

There are four sources that must be considered when teaching for success: the teacher, the student, the content, and the context. The interaction among these sources is important; each plays a role in the success of the teaching and learning process. On average, a teacher makes from one to six interactive decisions each hour during a typical day in the classroom. (Wilen, Ishler Bosse, Hutchison, & Kindsvatter, 2004). The teacher must constantly monitor and adjust the learning environment while maintaining an adequate standard for accomplishing the content objectives. Even the most accomplished teachers are challenged by the students who want to disrupt learning. This chapter will examine four sources to ensure success. First, teacher considerations are explained. Next we will look at learner considerations, including strategies for handling disruptive behaviors, followed by considerations regarding the content and finally the contextual influences under which instruction is delivered. In the summary section, recommendations for ensuring success with the teaching and learning process are provided.

Teacher Considerations to Ensure Success

Keep a Positive Outlook

Successful teachers must approach the teaching and learning process recognizing that they can and will make a difference in the lives of their students. Teachers must possess the outlook that all students can learn. Not many professions can promise as much reward and guarantee as much challenge as teaching. Not many experiences are as satisfying as being responsible for students' learning, for the satisfaction and pride that pours from the students when they finally get it. Yet few professions can pose such a threat to one's sense of self-efficacy. When students are disruptive, bored, or otherwise don't care, the challenges begin (Jensen, 1995). It is difficult to remain positive with the students who challenge us. However, accomplished teachers know that things can be tweaked to result in positive outcomes. Reflection is a part of every teacher's day. The process of reflection means thinking about what is working and not working. Reflection begins and ends with each lesson and with each interaction during the day. Teachers who blame themselves when students don't learn will fail a lot. Learning is not the sole responsibility of the teacher. In a classroom, the students are responsible for their learning; the teachers are responsible for facilitating that learning by finding the right strategies and methods to stimulate the students to learn. When students fail to learn, both the teacher and the students share in that failure. Teachers who reflect on an instructional lesson may ask these questions:

- Did the students learn?
- Did I select appropriate strategies?
- Did the students have the prerequisite knowledge?
- Was the environment conducive to learning? If not, why not?
- What do students need to do to contribute to their learning?
- Do the students understand their responsibility in learning?

If a teacher must reteach a lesson, how can he or she make that lesson be successful? Each "failure" in teaching occurs when the desired results are not achieved, but each "failure" informs the teacher about what does and does not work with the current group of students. Teaching at-risk students may largely be a trial-and-error routine. When teachers reflect and restructure, then real teaching has occurred. Teaching is just as much about the teacher's learning as it is about the students' learning. Each and every thing that is tried in the classroom eventually builds success. It adds to the knowledge necessary for success and increases the chances of the next event being more closely aligned with the desired outcomes.

In a sense, mistakes and failures become feedback that can be used to lead to classroom success. With many types of learners in the classroom, many techniques and strategies will be needed with plenty of flexibility. Each "failure" gets the teacher closer to the outcome, so the greater the flexibility, the greater the chance of a successful outcome. If this outlook becomes a part of the teacher's everyday life, imagine the excitement that can be generated. With each experience, positive or negative, a new gift can be discovered. The successes and failures of the job of teaching will constantly fluctuate. Once a teacher is hooked on the job of teaching, he or she becomes consumed by the complexity of the task and draws closer to the rewards of doing well for so many (Jensen, 1998). Learning to teach is a lesson in learning, and it requires a lifetime commitment. The teachers who accept the challenge will move forward to probe, to create, to stimulate, to challenge, to provoke, to think, and to care.

Use Effective Communication

The second teacher factor that influences success is communication. Communication skills can be divided into two categories: sending and receiving. Let's examine the sending skills used when speaking to someone else:

- Deal in the present. Information is more useful when it is shared at the earliest appropriate opportunity.
- Talk directly to students rather than about them. When teachers do this, students are shown respect and receive accurate information about adults' feelings.
- Speak courteously. This creates positive role models for students.
- Take responsibility for statements by using the personal pronoun "I." Example: "When I am interrupted, I get distracted and have difficulty helping other students."
- Make statements rather than asking questions. When dealing with students' behaviors, questions often create defensiveness. For example, "Tom, our classroom rules for participation are to raise your hand—I know you forgot because you were excited" rather than, "Tom, what is our rule for participating in class discussions?"

With regard to receiving communication, the techniques for becoming a more effective listener are important:

- Use empathic, nonevaluating listening. This makes the students feel that they have been clearly heard and that the feelings they express are acceptable.

- Use paraphrasing and active listening when responding to a student's contribution. Such techniques allow the students to become involved in the dialogue.
- Make eye contact and be aware of nonverbal messages.
- Suggest strong leadership with body carriage, facial expressions, and gestures.

Sending and receiving skills are important for teachers and students. They set the tone for the communication pattern that exists in the classroom. As a teacher, you can model appropriate speaking and listening skills for your students, regardless of their ages. Consider posting appropriate speaking and listening behaviors. Hang them in a permanent place in the classroom to help students learn how to have effective conversations.

Monitor the Classroom

The third teacher factor to ensure success is knowing how to effectively monitor the classroom. Consider the following tips:

- Scan the class frequently to notice and respond to potential problems.
- React calmly and quickly to a student's disruptive behavior to create a positive ripple effect.
- Make positive initial contact with students by praising the positive behavior that competes with the negative behavior.
- Remind students of the classroom rule or procedure that they are not demonstrating.
- Remind students of the rules and procedures and the consequence for violations.
- Give students clear cues indicating that continuation of inappropriate behavior will evoke the specified consequences.
- Employ consistent consequences for misbehaviors.
- Inform students that they are choosing the consequences for their behavior.
- Use consequences that are educational in nature. For example, if students have not completed their homework, they must look up two Internet sites on a topic relevant to the subject they are working on and write a description of what they have learned. (Use this sparingly, especially if the student views the computer time as fun.)
- When one or two students are being very disruptive, focus on the student demonstrating positive behavior. Then find a time to talk quietly with the disruptive students.

Facilitate Student Responsibilities for Learning

The final teacher factor to ensure success involves making students responsible for their learning. Responses to student misbehavior are most effective when they enhance the students' opportunities to be responsible for their behavior.

- Involve students in evaluating their own work as well as your instruction.
- Hand out an outline, definitions, lecture notes, or study guides to focus students' attention on the task at hand and to help organize their thoughts.
- Ask questions and give ample wait time before calling on the student. Wait time should last a minimum of three seconds after calling on a student and after a student has given their response.
- Vary the style as well as the content of instruction to address diverse student learning styles.
- Provide work of appropriate difficulty to complement varying ability levels.
- Relate materials to students' lives whenever possible.
- Be animated, create anticipation, and use activities to catch student interest or increase student motivation to participate.
- Engage student learning through cooperative group work, competitive teams, group discussions, debates, and role playing.

(Adapted from the Bureau of Education for Exceptional Students, Florida Department of Education, http://bsi.fsu.edu/)

Learner Considerations to Ensure Success

As teachers struggle to learn more about themselves and their students, many fears about students in relation to the learning process may result. Students often become bored in school, which leads to inattentive behaviors. In a survey of 25,000 eighth graders, students reported being bored in school half of the time (Rothman, 1990). Students find little connection between schoolwork and their lives outside of school. A gap exists between the students and the content to be learned, which in turn creates a gap between the teacher and the students in the classroom. When the gap between the teacher and the students occurs, teachers must refrain from labeling the students as "troublemakers" or "problem students." When students are unable to connect by behaving positively, they resort to misbehavior to achieve their goal. Intervention is needed to help these students, in addition to huge doses of encouragement. The difficulty for the teacher is that these students are often the ones that they feel least inclined to encourage. These are the "Teach me—I dare you" students.

Effective teachers know that these students want to belong and want to find their place in the group. As teachers reflect on the students who disrupt the classroom, they realize that the disruptive students are exhibiting one of four types of behavior: attention, power, revenge, or avoidance of failure (Albert, 1996). To understand the rationale behind students who disrupt the classroom, let's examine each of these four behaviors:

Attention. Some students disrupt because they are seeking ways to get attention. They want to be center stage all the time, and they constantly distract the teacher and the classmates to gain an audience.

Power. Some students want to have power over the teacher. They are seeking ways to boss. They want to exhibit their authority over the teacher, their classmates, and sometimes the whole class. At the very least, they want to show the other students that "you can't push me around." They refuse to comply with classroom rules or teacher requests and often disrupt the established order.

Revenge. The students who lash out to get even for real or imagined hurts are students who take their misbehavior to extremes. The target of revenge may be the teacher, other students, the school, or all of the above.

Avoidance of Failure. Some students want to avoid repeated failure. They cannot live up to the expectations of the teacher, their families, or even themselves. These are often the students who have potential but do not use it. To compensate for their feelings of failure, they choose withdrawal behaviors that make them appear inadequate or disabled.

These four sources of misbehavior were first noted by Dr. Rudolf Dreikurs in his observations of children, and they can provide valuable insight to teachers who reflect on the challenges proposed by disruptive students (Dreikurs, 1957, 1968). Whether the students' misbehavior is related to attention, power, revenge, or avoidance of failure, teachers are forced to respond. Strategies for responding to these students are summarized in the chart below. The first column lists the type of behavior, the middle column lists a general strategy to deal with the behavior, and the last column lists more specific techniques to use.

5.1. Cooperative Discipline Strategies

Behavior	General Strategy	Techniques
Attention-seeking behavior	Minimize the attention	Ignore the behavior Give "the eye" Stand close by Mention the student's name while teaching Send a secret notice
	Legitimize the behavior	Make a lesson out of the behavior Extend the behavior to its most extreme form Have your whole group join in the behavior
	Do the unexpected	Turn out the lights Lower your voice Change your voice Talk to the wall Cease talking temporarily
	Distract the student	Ask a direct question Ask a favor Change the activity
	Notice appropriate behavior	Thank students Write well-behaved students' names on board
	Move the student	Change the student's seat Send student to time out
Power and revenge behavior	Make a graceful exit	Acknowledge the student's power Remove the audience Table the matter Make a date Use a fogging technique: Agree with the student and change the subject
	Use time out	Assign time out in classroom, another room, a special room, office
	Set the consequences	Loss or delay of activity using objects or classroom materials or access to classroom/special activities Required interactions with others

Behavior	General Strategy	Techniques
Avoid-ance of failure	Modify instructional methods	Use concrete learning materials Teach one step at a time Cooperative groups
	Provide tutoring	Extra help from counselor Peer tutoring
	Teach positive self-talk	Post positive classroom signs Require two "put-ups" for every put-down Encourage positive self-talk before beginning tasks
	Make mistakes okay	Talk about mistakes Equate mistakes with effort Minimize the effect of making mistakes
	Build confidence	Focus on improvement Notice contributions Build on strengths Show faith in students Acknowledge the difficulty of a task Set time limits on tasks
	Focus on past success	Analyze past success Repeat past success
	Recognize achievement	Applause Clapping and standing ovations Awards

From *Cooperative Discipline*, by L. Albert, 1990, Circle Pines, MN: American Guidance Service.

Understanding the learner and the sources of misbehavior allows the teacher the opportunity to consider appropriate responses to disruptive behavior. When developing strategies for success, it becomes important for the teacher to know as much about the learner as is possible. Only when the learner is understood can teachers make wise decisions about how to respond.

Content Consideration to Ensure Success

Another source for ensuring success involves considerations about the content. The content can be controlled by the teacher or by the students, depending on the instructional strategy. Direct teaching is used when the aim of instruction is to communicate basic facts. This form of instruction is controlled by the teacher. Inquiry may be used when the teacher and the students are focused on an inductive process for learning content. Schooling should provide students insight into content knowledge, learning strategies, reasoning, logic, and a variety of specific processes and applications. Class activity should be conducted in a manner that gives students equal opportunities for learning the content. To enable student's equal access and opportunity, teachers must do more than provide one-sided lecture methods. The use of a variety of techniques can maximize the potential for student learning.

The teachers of Sunnybrook Middle School are planning for their annual fall festival. Each year the teachers structure activities and engage the students in an integrated thematic unit about fall and American colonial times. In the students' language arts class, they read and write about the Pilgrims. The students carve pumpkins in art class and make colorful construction paper turkeys. The social studies teacher has them develop a time line that extends across the room. The math teachers have students dunk for apples by counting and charting the results. In science, to replicate the time period, the students learn how to observe and collect data without using any forms of technology. A highlight of the thematic unit is a trip to a historic colony to observe actors portraying famous persons of the past.

In the case study above, the teachers did not identify outcome objectives to ensure that they are targeting necessary skills. It is one thing to plan fun activities, but the activities must be relevant, meaningful, and must have expected learning outcomes that are matched with the state or district curriculum goals. Teachers who plan interdisciplinary units must ask, "What is the focus for learning? What outcome objectives are intended?" When teachers begin to think about their content, they must match the standards from the state or district with the goals for learning. In the above example, how are the activities regarding the fall thematic unit compared to the state or district standards? What do the teachers expect the students to know and be able to do to demonstrate that learning has occurred? If teachers are a part of a team, they may have discussions regarding the activities that they plan in relation to the standard. In addition, it is important to examine learning outcomes in relation to the levels of thinking within the content to be taught. Content outcomes should be matched with Bloom's levels of thinking (Bloom, 1956).

Students are often curious about their world and things that surround them. This curiosity manifests itself in many ways. As students grow older, they become less curious about many learning tasks. Therefore, it becomes important for teachers to learn strategies that can arouse curiosity by presenting relevant content lessons.

Ms. McCoy is a busy first-year seventh-grade mathematics teacher in a rural community in the Midwest. She is happy about the progress that she has made with her students thus far. She feels lucky to be selected for her teaching position and she enjoys the team of teachers at her school. Waking up this November morning, she notices that snow had fallen during the night, and there is a damp, cold feeling to her apartment. She adjusts the thermostat in the hall on the way to the kitchen for her first cup of coffee. She reaches to turn on the television to the local news to find out whether schools have been closed. Hearing no school closings announced, Ms. McCoy begins to focus her attention on the events of the day. She knows that as a first-year teacher, her principal will be evaluating her progress and will be particularly interested in how well she manages the classroom. After having a conference with the principal yesterday, Ms. McCoy anticipates her first evaluation. The principal, Mr. Camacho, has told Ms. McCoy that she will be evaluated during her third-period class. Ms. McCoy begins to picture the students in this class in her mind's eye, realizing that there are at least three students in this class that are troublemakers. She begins to think through how she might handle these students as she quickly finishes her coffee, showers, and gets ready to leave. Just before locking the back door of her apartment to head for her car, she opens the utensil drawer in her kitchen. She reaches in and pulls out a spatula. Ms. McCoy has decided to use humor today as a way of introducing her math lesson and to gain her students' attention

As the third-period students begin to file in, Ms. McCoy notices Mr. Camacho taking a seat in the back of room. Now is the moment that she has rehearsed in her mind's eye. With the eyes of the students on her, Ms. McCoy pulls out the spatula from behind her back and says, "Okay, class, today we are going to flip some fractions." The students begin to chuckle…and Ms. McCoy smiles from ear to ear.

Not only did Ms. McCoy gain the attention of her students, she successfully evoked a humorous emotional response. An attention grabber or an anticipatory set is needed to begin a lesson if the students are not alert or "ready to go." Teachers know that establishing a routine to their instruction and creatively seeking ways to introduce new material make students curious about what will happen next. In a classroom like Ms. McCoy's, there is a sense of enjoyment felt by all and a sense of anticipation about what will happen next. Creating this positive classroom environment makes the lesson fun for the students, arouses their curiosity, and evokes an emotional response.

Good teachers know that students will attend to emotional things that matter. The question becomes, how do we get students charged emotionally to attend to the subjects we teach? Jensen (1998) designates five categories from which emotions can be derived. These instructional practices that evoke emotions can be incorporated when teaching content:

Movement

- Role-play theater, art, drama, mime, and simulations.
- Use music, instruments, debates, and cheers.
- Dance, play quiz show games, exercises, and stretch.
- Play, go on field trips, invite guest speakers.

Stakes

- Give students choices.
- Help students establish their goals.
- Allow opportunities for students to take part in public projects.

Novelty

- Allow students to videotape themselves as famous persons of the past.
- Convert the classroom to a rain forest, a futuristic city, a factory, a business, or another country.

Sharing

- Use cooperative learning environments where students develop mutual trust, share materials, discuss, and debate learning activities.
- Establish a positive classroom climate where students support one another.

Apprenticeships

- Develop service learning projects that help students develop relationships with experts or community agencies.
- Use big brother and big sister systems within the school.
- Implement multiage classrooms.

Complex Projects

- Do fewer but more complex projects.
- Evoke curiosity, mystery, excitement, and challenge by integrating the skills of math, science, problem solving, and research.

Each of the above suggestions can strengthen content to ensure success. Another important part of ensuring success is understanding the fine line between challenge and making assignments too easy. Let's examine this distinction in the next section.

Considerations About the Context for Instruction

Challenge of the Assignment

Students should be given assignments that are challenging, not too easy. Challenge does not mean assigning 20 problems instead of 15. Increasing the amount of work that students complete and overloading students with busy-work is not providing challenge. There is a fine line between this difference, and it varies with each situation, each student, and each context under which instruction is delivered. Students who lag behind others may need some special assistance. This is particularly true if the students are non–English speaking or have mental or physical challenges. In these situations, teachers can tap the resources available to them in their districts to get assistance with these special populations. However, if a student lacks motivation, it may be necessary for the teacher to provide an alternative assignment. Teachers may want to adjust a writing assignment around students' interests. Teachers will be able to assess the students' writing proficiency but allow them the opportunity to explore their areas of interest.

Teachers who provide an error-proof classroom are not challenging the students enough. Teachers may reduce task difficulty, overlook errors, and de-emphasize failed attempts. The best way to promote a challenging environment for learning is by holding high standards for your students and by talking to them about their mistakes. Help them understand that mistakes are not an indication of low intelligence but rather are attempts to make things better. Everyone makes mistakes, and when mistakes occur, it is a lesson in learning. Continue to boost students' confidence by seeking ways to have them discover where they are on the continuum between challenging and easy tasks.

The context within each learning task is an important consideration to ensure success. Not every lesson is the same, because not every student or experience is the same. Therefore, the context under which instruction occurs is highly variable. To assist with the context under which instruction is delivered, consider these organizational procedures:

- Arrange seating in a U shape, rows, or a circle for easy access and eye contact with students.
- Post a daily schedule and discuss any changes each morning.
- Engage students until you have given clear instructions for the upcoming activity.
- Encourage students to take responsibility for their learning by determining not to do tasks that can be done by students.

- Establish routines for collecting homework, distributing papers, and so on.
- Move around the room and attend to individual needs.
- Provide simple step-by-step directions for any new activity or assignment.
- Remind students of key procedures associated with the upcoming lesson.
- Use group competition to stimulate more orderly transitions.
- Develop transition activities.

Alter the Students' Working Environment and Use Peer Tutoring and Cooperative Learning

Socialization is important to the young adolescent. Teachers should structure lessons so that students can learn socialization in the form of cooperative group arrangements. Sharing material, taking turns, listening to other points of view, and collaborating with each other to solve problems are worthy goals for instruction. Teachers must learn to structure tasks so that individual accountability and group goals are both achieved. This means changing the work environments for the students. Vary the format of the lesson and allow students to engage in learning opportunities that include group and individual arrangements.

Make Learning Relevant to Students

Mr. Parker is an eighth-grade American history teacher in a large suburban middle school. During the last period of the day, while the students are completing a written assignment, he begins to plan for the next unit of study on the Civil War. He is excited to think about this unit because it represents his favorite time in American history. He begins to think of all the resources he can bring to class to share with the students. He knows the library near his home has some Civil War relics, and he is aware of the resources in his school's media center. As he begins to plan for his first day, he decides to spend time on the political and military aspects or the war. On the following Monday, Mr. Parker begins his lesson with a 20-minute overview of the Civil War and the important leaders. During Mr. Parker's explanation, Juan and Miguel are watching a squirrel on the windowsill of the classroom. Mr. Parker is so interested in what he is saying that he does not notice the squirrel or Juan and Miguel. Juan is now tapping Miguel's leg as the squirrel bobs its head up and down. Pretty soon both Miguel and Juan begin bobbing their heads to mimic the squirrel. The other students in the row begin to laugh. Mr. Parker has not a clue why.

Teachers assume that something that is relevant to them will be relevant to the students. This is not the case. When teachers begin their lesson, they announce the objective of the day to the students: "Today we will discuss the Civil War." After hearing this, despite the teacher's enthusiasm for his subject matter, students' eyes roll to the back of their heads and boredom sets in. Whatever the plan that a teacher may have for a lesson, if it does not connect with the learner, little is retained. Instead of paying attention, the learners become distracted and begin to misbehave. As well intentioned as the teacher may be, or as well planned as the lesson may be, if it is not relevant to the student, it is not learned.

Teachers can adjust the learning task so that students can become more curious. They can also balance the level of difficulty of the assignment and find connections with their students' lives by making the material relevant. Understanding the sources of student motivation and considering these elements will help promote an understanding of student interest and needs.

Summary

This chapter has outlined the role of the teacher, student, content, and context regarding instructional delivery. Teachers who are faced with at-risk learners must take into account each of these essential components.

Teachers know that when students learn, they construct their own meaning for an experience through their interaction with the event, object, person, idea, or activity. Each person has a different set of background experiences, and each person's construction or interpretation of the experience will be somewhat different. A balance needs to be maintained between the teaching and learning process. Even the students who dare us can benefit from the following set of recommendations for the establishment of successful classrooms, which are based on all the previous information presented in this chapter:

- ◆ **Use less whole-class, teacher-directed instruction.** With the pressure to cover the content and prepare students for standardized tests, there has been a return to direct instruction. Direct instruction works best with basic facts and low-level knowledge and skills. However, direct instruction does not work with students at risk. This pattern of instruction is familiar to them because it is overused by teachers. Teachers who break the cycle of direct instruction will facilitate opportunities for students to learn. The eighth-grade student who is not listening may be bored with the mundane direct instruction approach and will block out what is supposed to be learned. This is because with direct instruction, students are seated, passive, and simply expected to receive and absorb information. This separates the students from their learning. Consider the use of instructional techniques that promote curiosity, excitement, and motivation. Pre-expose students to the topics to be learned. Discover what your students' interests and background are and allow your students to set goals for learning. Make the learning environment colorful and exciting. State strong positive expectations.

◆ **Grab their attention.** Vary your voice tone or use a poem, a riddle, a jingle, or a product logo. The point is to grab your student's attention. Attention grabbers stimulate student interest in the learning task. One middle-grade teacher who consistently used attention grabbers had students speculating and predicting their teacher's techniques on the way to school.

◆ **Make it relevant.** If students need to ask, "Why do we need to know this?" they are not understanding content relevance. State a purpose for the each learning lesson and tell the students what you expect them to be able to accomplish following each teaching segment. Take time to explore students' prior knowledge before teaching a new concept of skill. Become an expert in creating bridges from students' past experience to new learning.

◆ **Make less of an attempt to thinly "cover" large amounts of material.** Make sure that when you plan your lessons, they are connected to a larger goal with specific learner outcomes. To just cover the material by week nine of the school year is not effective learning. Anything worth knowing needs reflection and may take time. It is better to learn one thing from three different perspectives then it is to cover 10 things and forget everything learned after one month has passed.

◆ **Teach students in teams or groups.** Two to five students working together can generate more ideas, more examples, and deeper understanding. Utilize the social needs of the students for added motivation. Many students will work harder for the success of a peer group then they would working alone. Rotate teams regularly. Practice teaching the interpersonal and social skills associated with group work. Allow group members to build trust and encourage them to correct their own mistakes.

◆ **Teach goal setting.** Encourage students to set their own realistic goals. Teachers can help by probing students, "Tell me how many paragraphs you will write today? I bet you can write five paragraphs." Use these as stepping stones to larger achievements.

- **Keep it visual.** Teach students to monitor and graph their progress toward the goals that they select. Simple graphs provide excellent visual displays and documentation of students' progress. Use a variety of visual and graphic organizers to assist with student understanding. Charts, diagrams, and semantic webs allow students to find connections among the concepts to be learned.

- **Stimulate the cognitive.** Use "think-alouds" as you demonstrate the steps of a new procedure or process. Tell students exactly what you are thinking and allow them to hypothesize the next steps.

- **Use mnemonic techniques.** Use these techniques to improve memory. In some cases, first=letter acrostics may be devised, such as HOMES, in which each letter represents the name of the Great Lakes (Huron, Ontario, Michigan, Erie, and Superior). Other memory techniques like the link word method can be used.

- **Keep the action going.** Employ active learning techniques. Small dry-erase boards or individual chalkboards or game boards provide excellent opportunities for guided practice. Teach students to take lecture notes using a series of guided steps. Provide a structured outline of the lesson and have students fill in the blanks. Gradually decrease the amount of information you provide so they learn how to write their own good notes.

- **Practice, practice, practice.** Provide lots of opportunities for students to practice a new skill. These can take the form of coaching activities (e.g., "Turn to your neighbor and share two things." "Tell your buddy." "Show the person on your left." "Read to your partner.").

- **Provide closure.** Use specific closure activities. Have students learn the skills to synthesize, summarize, and to conclude (e.g., "Before you leave, tell me two important things you learned today." "Summarize in one sentence what you learned about." "Before the bell we have just enough time to name the steps we learned today.") After learning has taken place, provide systematic review for the content you teach. Even the most interesting and motivating instruction will not be remembered unless systematic review takes place.

To minimize the challenges provided by the students who dare us, use techniques when you instruct that help you meet the needs of the students and accomplish lessons in learning. This chapter has reviewed the essential components for teaching for success: the teacher, the student, the content, and the context. Not every lesson will be effective for every learner. One size does not fit all. However, by employing the strategies that have been provided, the outcomes for success are ensured.

Resources and References

Albert, L. (1996). *Cooperative discipline.* Circle Pines, MN: American Guidance Service.

Belanca, J., & Fogarty, R (1995).. *Blueprints for thinking in the cooperative classroom.* Palatine, Illinois: Skylight Publishing.

Berlyne, D. E. (1960). *Conflict, arousal, and curiosity.* New York: Mc Graw Hill.

Bloom, B. (Ed.). (1956). *A taxonomy of educational objectives. Handbook I: Cognitive domain.* New York: McKay.

Conyers, M., & Wilson, D. *Research-Based Graduate Education & Professional Development: Top 10 ways to Turn on Your Superbrain*: Retrieved July 12, 2003, www.brainsmart.com

Davis, B., Sumara, D., & Luce-Kapler. R. (2000). *Engaging minds: Learning and teaching in a complex world.* Mahwah, NJ: Erlbaum Associates, Inc.

Diegmueller, K. (1996). *Running out of steam. Thoughtful teachers, thoughtful schools.* Boston: Allyn and Bacon.

Dreikurs, R. (1957, 1958). *Psychology in the classroom.* New York: Harper & Row.

Fulk, B. (2000). Make instruction more memorable. *Intervention in School and Clinic, 35*(3), 183–184.

Goodstein, M. (2004). Everyday Study Skills. *Instructor* (114) 2, 43–48.

Hootstein, E. W. (1994). Enhancing student motivation: Make learning interesting and relevant. *Education,* 14 (3), 475.

Hunter, M. (1994). *Enhancing Teaching.* New York: Macmillan College Publishing.

Jensen, E. (1995). *Super teaching.* Del Mar, CA: Turning Points for Teachers.

Jensen, E. (1998). *Teaching with the brain in mind.* Alexandria, VA: ASCD.

Kohn, A. (2004) *What does it mean to be well educated?* Boston: Beacon Press.

Kroll, L. R., & Galguera, T. (2005). *Teaching and learning to teach as principled practice.* Thousand Oaks, CA: Sage.

LeDoux, J. (1996). *The emotional brain.* New York: Simon and Schuster.

Mitchell, M. (1993). Situational interest: Its multifaceted structure in the secondary school mathematics classroom. *Journal of Educational Psychology,* 85(3), 424–436.

Rallis, S., Rossman, G, Phlegar, J., & Abeille, A. (1995). *Dynamic teachers leaders of change.* Thousand Oaks, CA: Corwin Press.

Rosenshine, B. (1983). Teaching functions in instructional programs. *Elementary School Journal,* 83 (4), 335–351.

Rothman, R. (1990, November 17). Educators focus on ways to boost student motivation. *Education Week,* (10), 11–13.

Schiefele, U. (1991). Interest, learning, and motivation. *Educational Psychologist,* 26(3–4), 299–323.

Sprenger, M. (1999). *Learning and memory. The brain in action.* Alexandria: VA Association for Supervision and Curriculum Development.

Wilen, W., Ishler Bosse, M., Hutchison, J., & Kindsvatter, R. (2004). *Dynamics of effective secondary teaching* (5th ed.). Boston: Pearson/A and B.

Wolfe, P. (2001). *Brain matters.* Alexandria, Va: Association for Supervision of Curriculum and Development (ASCD).

Wood, K. (2004). *Interdisciplinary instruction. A practical guide for elementary and middle school teachers.* Columbus, OH: Pearson Merrill Prentice Hall.

Zemelman, S., Daniels, H., & Hyde, A. (1998). *Best practice: New standards for teaching and learning in America's schools* (2nd ed.). Portsmouth, NH: Heinemann.

6

Intervening with Those Who Dare Us

Jesse's name was at the top of the list on the principal's desk. Lack of attendance, lack of homework, and a poor attitude required that something be done immediately.

As there are levels and degrees of risk in each school, there are levels and degrees of intervention. The intervention must match the type of risk behavior being demonstrated. Those adults most closely connected to the student who dares us to teach him or her must communicate with each other and the student and create a plan of action for behavioral change. A plan of action is not something that is done *to* the at-risk student but done *with the input of* the student. If the student does not own the intervention, it will be a waste of time and no true change will take place.

Classroom Interventions

Classroom interventions can be as simple as changing where a student sits in the classroom, having a one-on-one conference with the student, analyzing the reading ability of a student, having a conference with parents, or modeling proper behavior in group settings. However, they usually are more complex when the student is interacting with a group of peers. In many different interviews with at-risk students, the students suggest that any classroom intervention be discussed privately with them instead of embarrassing them in front of their peers. If action is taken in front of a group, the student must first deal with their concerns about what their peers are thinking and may miss the entire point of the teacher's intervention. Too often, teachers become frustrated by a student's lack of attention, lack of work completed, poor attitude, or inappropriate behavior and react without a plan. Removing the student from the class is the first response of many teachers, and that may be a positive reward rather than a negative one. Some students will dare you to teach them just to get out of a certain class. Perhaps they are not prepared; perhaps there is something else going on in their lives; perhaps they are gifted and bored. Nevertheless, once they are removed from the class, the problem has been avoided, not solved.

Kyle began his eighth-grade year with a promise to himself that this would be the year he would try to achieve academically and change his reputation. In seventh grade he had joined with a group of troublemakers, and although he had never been in trouble, he was judged by the company he kept. Teachers did not expect much from him and he soon lowered his work level to their expectations. He lived with his grandparents, who had very little control over his actions.

As he grew physically, several teachers and coaches encouraged him to participate in athletics. Unfortunately, his group of friends didn't like the kids who were athletes, so he chose not to even try. Perhaps this was the year he would play basketball. He had spent the summer helping his grandfather on the farm and fishing. On the occasions when he went to town with his group, he was urged to drink and use drugs. He gave in to peer pressure on two occasions and struggled to stay out of serious trouble.

He loved math, but because he had not tried in seventh grade, he had been placed in a class far below his ability level. He was in a class with most of the "low achievers" that were in his social group. The math teacher gave a comprehensive pre-assessment to the class and he scored in the top 2% of all students. This discrepancy caused the math teacher to look at the standardized tests that had been given in the past four years to this young man, and she soon saw that this was a case of a classic underachiever who had been placed in the wrong class.

The very astute teacher also informed the basketball coach that this young man could well be hiding some real talent. Both the teacher and the coach made this young man their personal goal for the year, and they were not disappointed. Their interventions were timely, consistent, and based on factual ability data that they used to boost the self-image of this student.

The classroom teacher is usually the first person to realize the level of risk for a student. Classroom behaviors, grades, attendance, attitude, and interaction with peers give clues that enable a teacher to intervene in the school life of the student whose countenance says, "Teach me—I dare you."

The School Culture

When students enter a school, they enter a culture. The culture consists of values, beliefs, artifacts, and communication. This culture can be perceived to be supportive or nonsupportive to the at-risk student. Most at-risk students attend a regular middle or high school and sit in classrooms just like their peers. They look like the rest of the students, and they try to blend in and not call attention to their learning difficulties. They may have been doing that for years. Some actually excel in extracurricular activities or out-of-school endeavors but struggle in the classroom. Within the culture of their school, "Teach me—I dare you" students may only be noticed by one teacher in one subject area. Many times their needs are not known by their peers, their parents, or their other teachers. When they are known, some actions are discreetly taken by administrators and counselors to protect them and keep them in school and learning.

One middle school principal recognized that many of the students in the school came to school in clothing that had an offensive odor and was ill-fitting. This lack of material essentials kept capable students from participating in class or extracurricular activities. These students lived in homes that often had no hot water for washing themselves or their clothing.

The principal asked local radio stations, businesses, and service groups to donate new T-shirts that were used for their advertising. Some donated sweatshirts, and others donated money to be used to buy sweatpants and gym clothes. The response from the community was generous, and the collection of new clothing was enough to offer new clothes to kids at least twice a week.

Every student in the school signed up for a "good behavior" drawing on Monday, and those who had not been sent to the office for discipline infractions could put their name in. Every Wednesday the principal drew several names, and the winners got a new T-shirt. He made sure that the students who had no clean clothes were frequent winners. It was a small but important effort to help these students. He also made school showers available before school for any student who needed to use them.

This intervention was carefully thought out by the leadership in the building so that no student would be embarrassed but all would have access to the basic items for cleanliness. Careful planning by administrators, counselors, and teachers is a key ingredient of intervention. Too many reactive interventions have had the opposite effect from what was intended.

Other interventions have involved having community mentors as a part of a specific class project. Projects such as the Veterans History Project (sponsored by the American Folklife Center of the Library of Congress, www.loc.gov/vets/vets-home.html) for history classes involve students in the interviews and documentation of war experiences of veterans. Students who may not respond to traditional teaching methods in history seem to change their entire attitude when involved in a project that requires them to do something important. Projects that require job shadowing and community service involve students with other adults who may serve as role models not only for behavior but for future goal setting.

Interventions that are designed to target specific skill development, such as the Higher Order Thinking Skills (HOTS) Program (www.hots.org), have high success rates but can require specific teacher training. These programs usually are designed to improve reading, math, or thinking skills.

Community interventions include home visitations by teachers and administrators, community center outreach programs, family service projects, and community support groups. Counselors at all levels of schooling should make themselves aware of the available resources in their communities and provide a guide book for teachers, parents, and students.

If possible, a school-community committee of representative groups should be established to develop a comprehensive plan for helping students both in and out of school. One simple task for that type of group can be the development of a school textbook shelf at the local public library. If teachers would place a copy of each required text on that shelf as a reference, students would have access to the books outside of school hours.

Presentations by local drug and alcohol prevention programs can be planned by a school community committee. These presentations can offer students accurate information about the biological aspects of drug and alcohol use, legal issues, and decisions about use. They can also provide resources for students to get help outside of school. The goal is to give students the facts they need to make good choices about those issues. Community groups are eager to meet with students and welcome invitations from the school

Proactive Interventions

Interventions can be made for individual students, specific groups of students, or the entire school. What is important is that they be proactive and based on needs of students. Proactive interventions are designed to help students before they become at risk. Some examples include the programs and classes in our school that teach students about decision making, goal setting, problem solving, and social interaction. They cover topics like dating, sex, drugs, health, careers, tough decisions, and other hot topics of student interest.

Proactive interventions also include information given to classroom teachers about students' abilities. Information may include reading scores, health needs, prior remediation, and general comments by previous teachers. Proactive interventions can take the form of counseling groups or classes that provide students with skills and resources for living their entire lives. Counselors design these support groups whenever the need arises with a group of students.

Many schools provide interventions with clubs related to content areas. These clubs are informal in nature and allow students to explore their interests with a teacher who shares a passion for that subject. Science, reading, math, and language clubs are very popular. Many physical education teachers are designing walking clubs to try to help more adolescents exercise. The walking clubs meet at lunch and after school, and the participants set goals and walk together to reach those goals.

Remedial Interventions

The students who are brought to the attention of the classroom teacher prior to the beginning of school are usually those who have been placed in special programs, have special physical or emotional needs, or have been held back in one or more classes for failure to complete the work. They need continuation of their special programs and additional attention from mentors. Although every adolescent can use the skills of a mentor, these students need mentors who are consistent and continuous.

Mentors

Mentors can be found throughout the school and the community. There are skilled retirees, business owners, professionals, parents, service clubs, and college students who can all be invited to mentor a student. Mentors can also be older students who mentor younger students. Mentors should be given a brief training program on how they can best help students. Some will come to the school to help, whereas others will offer job opportunities, assistantships, and apprenticeships in the community. The school should set the goals for the mentoring program so that the continuity and consistency that students need is understood and provided by all. Principals mentor several students per year, both formally and informally. When a list is compiled of the neediest students in a school, all adults in the building should have at least one student to mentor. High school students can mentor middle and elementary school students, and middle school students can mentor in the elementary school. There are several essential steps in designing a mentoring program:

1. Compile a pool of names of people and businesses that will help. Start by asking service organizations and churches in the community to inform their members of the need.

2. Set the goals for the program for the first year.

3. Send a letter of invitation to those people explaining exactly what they will be asked to do. Ask them what other skills they can bring to the mentoring process.

4. Match students with mentors and select a time in the student's schedule when the mentoring will take place.

5. Train the mentors in how to help these students and inform them of any special materials that will be used.

6. Hold an initial meeting of the mentor and the mentee with a very specific success goal (e.g., the mentor will help the mentee complete all of the reading for history class for this week).

7. Give everyone involved a schedule of mentoring times.

8. Recognize the work of both mentors and mentees with regular notes and updates.

9. For those mentors who cannot meet with students during school hours, have them tape textbooks, meet after school, or provide phone or e-mail support to the student. Many businesses will offer career training to several students if the partnership with the school is monitored by the administration.

10. Have students and mentors evaluate the process after the first three meetings and supply needed interventions to make it successful.

Making a Plan of Action

There are a large number of students who are not brought to the early attention of the teacher and have had no interventions. These students may become increasingly at risk over the summer or school year because of some family change. Knowing when and how to intervene and refer are skills required of every classroom teacher. Teachers may become overwhelmed and burned out over the multitude of problems that their students face. Poverty, abuse, drug use, teen pregnancy, and unrealistic expectations for an entire group of students may create an atmosphere of hopelessness. If teachers attempt to help the entire population of at-risk students, the task can seem overwhelming. That is why a plan of action is needed by the school district and why resources must be identified before large-scale actions are taken.

Teachers should remember to start with one student at a time. Take the student's dare to teach them, and then conference with that student to make a plan of action. When social issues get in the way of academic participation, the teacher should go with the student as an academic advocate to the counselor or resource person who might be able to help. When entire groups of students are affected by serious risk, the school should form a group of teachers, students, parents, community personnel, and administrators to peruse available resources for the group and establish a plan of action.

Curricular Interventions

There are numerous examples of successful intervention programs that have been specific to one school or a regional group of schools. There are programs that have targeted specific skills such as reading and math for at-risk students that have been successful. Almost every classroom teacher has a success story to share about a student (and should be encouraged to do so), and community agencies have designed specific programs to help these students in the after-school hours.

Outdoor education and survival programs such as Outward Bound (www.outwardbound.org) have been highly successful in motivating at-risk students. Schools that provide their own outdoor education programs have consistently seen at-risk students achieve and lead in a setting other than the school. Schools that require and provide community service activities for their students have seen the "Teach me—I dare you" students connect with senior citizens, animals, and the environmental needs of their area.

Within the curriculum of any school there are choices for teachers and students to make. Interdisciplinary units have been one way in which middle school has dealt with special topics of interest of their students. One middle school, concerned about the lack of social skills of their students, did an entire unit on manners. They included all subject areas and all students, covering the history of manners, table manners, phone manners, group manners, concert manners, conversational manners, and special occasion manners. The students, in groups, did research on manners, and the unit culminated in a formal afternoon tea for the teachers and Board of Education. Every student had a part in making the afternoon a success. Some made invitations in art, some planned background music, some made cookies and tea, and others greeted guests in a receiving line, generated appropriate conversation, made sure everyone was served properly, and made wooden place card holders. Teachers were astounded at the outcome of the unit, and the unit as an intervention carried over into the rest of the school year.

Other curriculum interventions include conflict resolutions classes, decision making classes, and reading and writing across the curriculum.

Programs that teach specific skills such as Operation Respect (www.dontlaugh.org) and HOTS programs are designed to address certain goals and behaviors. They help students develop skills that keep them in school and out of trouble. They work at developing a culture of caring.

High-Ability At-Risk Students

Curriculum for high-ability at-risk students is offered both in the classroom and in pull-out programs. Gifted students who are impatient, sarcastic, or disruptive often dare the classroom teacher to not only teach them but challenge them as well. They find assignments boring because they learn nothing new. Allowing gifted students to complete alternate assignments or independent study has been successful in keeping those students on task and motivated in the classroom. The curriculum should be modified for gifted at-risk students in their areas of strength.

If the student who is gifted can complete regular assignments without difficulty, a plan of alternate assignments and projects should be written by the student and the teacher together. Students who are gifted but at risk should not be placed in cooperative groups with students who need drill and practice. Those activities frustrate gifted learners, who feel like they end up teaching everyone in their group. Gifted students should be given more challenging tasks during regular drill-and-practice class sessions. Students can be both learning disabled and gifted, so accurate identification measures are necessary. Teachers must be given training in identification of gifted students as well as those who have obvious learning problems.

Successful Interventions from Successful Teachers

A summary of the suggestions from a variety of schools, research studies, and personal interviews with successful teachers includes the following interventions to use with "Teach me—I dare you" students to give them the ability and dignity they need to survive:

♦ Survey and interview students often to assess their needs and progress. Ask questions like these: What is the best idea you had this week? What do you have questions about in science? What did you learn this week that made you want to learn more? If you could have help in one thing, what would it be?

- Evaluate your curriculum from an at-risk point of view. Is it too much, too soon? Too high a reading level for some? Too much to be done outside of class? Ask students to give feedback on the material.

- Provide language experiences that include basic reading skills such as phonetics for poor readers. Give opportunities to read and write often with immediate feedback and assistance. Offer high-interest magazines and books at a variety of reading levels. Assess reading skills accurately by using a reading skill test.

- Reinforce any gains with a personal positive comment and a note home if appropriate. Call parents to let them know that students are making progress.

- Teach study skills and test-taking strategies. Design tests that are able to be divided into sections for alternate completion times for slower readers. Have students write a test about material they have read. Have them take their own test. Share tests with other students and let them practice taking their tests. The design of the tests will tell a teacher what the students thought was important and what material they may have missed.

- Use teaching teams that share students, meeting regularly to discuss them. Both core and exploratory teachers should be on teams that discuss students. Counselors and administrators should attend all meetings where students are discussed or at least receive minutes of the meetings. Teams should set aside one meeting a week to talk about students. They should address all students on the team and focus on what is working with kids at risk.

- Assess student learning styles and multiple intelligences. Use that information to design a variety of ways for students to meet the learning objectives.

- Teach concretely with models of quality work and connections to the teenage culture. Show students what good work looks like.

- Encourage and assign group homework projects.

- Organize opportunities to have students witness and practice compassion. Reading to younger children, writing cards for the elderly, serving donuts and hot chocolate to hungry peers, and having an advisory session on how to express sympathy are all examples from middle and high schools.

- Require less busywork and more quality in what is completed.

- Check progress of "Teach me—I dare you" students daily.

◆ Read to students. Even if it is only for five minutes, the students will enjoy the time when all they have to do is listen.

◆ Provide ways for students to get caught up without embarrassing them. Send notes to those who are far behind offering a time and place to meet so that you can help them get organized to get caught up. High schools that have seminar and advisory programs simply encourage students to seek out a teacher they need to see at this time. No one is singled out when the opportunity is available to all.

◆ Avoid sarcasm and ridicule in the classroom.

◆ Help the students develop a vision of what they can become by offering successful role models in class and in the community.

◆ Provide mentors for all students who need motivation, assistance, and an adult to listen to them. Mentors can come from within the school or from the community. There are many senior citizens available in every community who would help students if they were invited and given some basic training.

◆ Use one-on-ones as a regular means of checking with students. Using the process of one-on-one intervention requires that the adult use the techniques of active listening, paraphrasing, alternative actions searches, goal setting, evaluation, and checking back.

Although there are many more suggestions from students and teachers, the most effective strategy may be taking the time to listen to students.

Interventions for High-Risk Students

There are high risks such as alcohol and drug use, chronic truancy, sexual activity, and violence that require far more intervention than can be given by the classroom teacher, but the teacher is always the most available on a daily basis to notice changes in behaviors and learning patterns that may be indicative of increasing risk for students. If the school has a counselor, social worker, or counseling staff, they are normally the next level of intervention. They are connected to a variety of community and state agencies that can intervene in nonacademic-related risk cases.

There are groups within each community that have resources for helping students at risk from alcohol, drugs, sexual activity, and violence. It is often difficult for the classroom teacher to know what help is available when the "Teach me—I dare you" attitude is caused by substance abuse, neighborhood issues, or a family problem. Counselors and administrators can make a directory of resource agencies in their community available to students and teachers. Some schools post the toll-free numbers of agencies on the board in every room, in the cafeteria, and in the bathrooms.

Interventions for "Teach Me—I Dare You Students" Who Are Discipline Problems

In a study (Bergmann, 1989) of students most frequently sent to the office for discipline problems, principals noted that those repeat visitors frequently did not have a positive and supportive home environment. In one middle school used in the study, the following students were at risk:

- One student came to school only when a court order was obtained.
- One student had moved seven times within a year.
- Several students had total responsibility for younger siblings before and after school.
- Several students were facing court dates on truancy and vandalism charges.
- Two students had parents who were in prison.
- Several boys admitted that they purposely tried to get sent to the principal's office because they would then have someone to talk with them.

These students are a microcosm of the larger population in many urban communities. All of these students required interventions beyond those given by the classroom teacher. The family problems of the students may overwhelm them until they are unable to participate in school. There is a point when "Teach me—I dare you" turns to "Help me cope with this impossible situation." At that point, the teacher and counselor or social worker must call in those resources that deal with social issues. Local city and county agencies including the health department, social services, and court liaisons are usually the first resources called.

Successful Intervention Programs Outside of the School

Historically, there have been many intervention programs that were offered to students at risk. Some of these, like Outward Bound, had high success rates with at-risk students. Other programs that teach decision making, problem solving, or career preparation have also been successful with certain types of students. Successful intervention programs have separated at-risk students from other students, offered a work experience, provided intensive counseling and support, focused on a nontraditional curriculum with many hands-on activities, and found ways to help students feel supported. Vocational programs, apprenticeships, and work study have also been offered as alternatives for at-risk students.

Health Issues

Although health issues are at the top of the list of concerns of most teens, fewer and fewer schools are offering consistent information or classes on health issues. The "Teach me—I dare you" students often have health issues that affect their attitude, attendance, and achievement in school. Those who lack sleep, get little or no exercise, use drugs or alcohol, or have undiagnosed conditions such as diabetes, asthma, or sexually transmitted disease need interventions by a health professional in addition to accurate information. Most schools require a physical examination for participation in athletics, but not for students in general.

One of the first questions that should be asked about students who have a sudden drop in grades, change in attitude, or recurrent attendance issues is, "Have they had a physical examination in the past year?" Counselors and administrators should work with parents and the local health department to ensure that these students are offered medical attention and advice. Accurate drug and alcohol information should be made available to these students.

One middle school asked a panel of local doctors, lawyers, and police officers to come to the school and answer any questions that the students had about health, drugs, alcohol, and the law. Students and teachers submitted their questions ahead of time. Students were allowed to ask additional questions during the assembly also. Only the counselors and school nurse were present during the session. Students respected the information given by the professionals, and many of the at-risk students asked for additional help after that session.

First Steps in Intervention

When in doubt as to how to intervene to help students, the first and sometimes only step is to conference with them privately and ask them. Most of the time that conference will give students the opportunity to have someone listen to them, a chance to outline their difficulties, an opportunity to make a plan of action, and the knowledge that someone cares. Sometimes it takes two or three conferences for a student to tell you how he or she needs help, but knowing that a teacher cares remains the most effective way to begin to take the dare given by the student.

Intervention Suggestions for Parents

Parents may be the most frustrated by their child who dares us to teach them. Usually their efforts have been ongoing and supportive during the elementary years, but they become overwhelmed when confronted by the number of teachers in the middle and high school. As expectations change from those of one teacher to those of many, at-risk students may slowly withdraw from the schooling process without any attention for a long period of time. A failing progress report or a phone call home may be the first evidence a parent has that their child is in academic trouble.

The familiar "What did you do in school today?" answered by the all-too-familiar "Nothing" is a routine that needs to be changed. Parents can ask, "What was the best part of your day today?" or "Tell me one thing you learned in your classes today" or "What part of today would you liked to have changed?" These questions require more thought and a more involved response than the traditional "Nothing."

Parent involvement in a child's education is seen as key to student success. When students feel like their parents care, they are more apt to care about their work. As students develop through the teen years, keeping the lines of communication open is imperative. Parents should make an effort to know their child's teachers and read communications from the school.

Parents can ask the teachers to communicate with them about their child on a regular basis if the child is having difficulty in a subject area. They should be made aware of assignments, due dates, and expectations for completion of work. If parents suspect that drugs, alcohol, or gang behavior may be a part of their child's diminished success in school, they can talk with the school counselor, social worker, or a community agency that deals with particular teen issues. Asking for information and help is the first essential step in helping their student succeed. Parents can also volunteer to help in the school by serving as mentors, readers, resource collectors, or chaperones. They can help teachers develop a resource list of parent helpers and what they can provide.

Communicating and working together to help a student succeed can be hard work, especially if the student initially refuses help. Few students really want to fail, and their challenges are attempts to obtain help for whatever is obstructing their learning. Parents, teachers, administrators, counselors, and community agencies must be willing to try several kinds of interventions if necessary to keep a student in school and learning. One size does not fit all, and one intervention may not be enough for students who dare us to teach them. The resources listed at the end of this chapter include successful programs and practices that have been used in classrooms with students who are at risk. In every school there is a teacher who is able to connect with these students. Sometimes that teacher is very demanding, sometimes that teacher is very understanding, but all teachers who can reach at-risk students seem to have high standards and truly believe that these students can learn. The strategy that makes them different is that they intervene by listening to the students. That is the starting point for all interventions.

References and Resources

Bergmann, S. (1989). *Discipline and guidance—The thin line in the middle school.* Reston, VA: NASSP.

Search Institute, The. (1997). *The asset approach: Giving kids what they need to succeed* [Booklet]. Minneapolis, MN: Author.

Websites Related to Intervention

www.edjj.org/focus/prevention/phcsc.html
www.edp.msu.edu/publications/accountability/at-risk.htm
http://hots.org/index.html
www.hots.org/articles.html
www.mathematica-mpr.com/Press%20Releasess/qop.asp
www.nasponline.org/publications/cq262high_ability.html
www.ncrel.org/sdrs/areas/issues/students/atrisk/at500.htm
www.search-institute.org

Federal Intervention Programs for At-Risk Students

www.ericdigests.org/1998-1/door.htm
www.coin3.com/funding/esea.htm
www.ncrel.org/sdrs/areas/issues/students/atrisk/at800.htm
www.sharingsuccess.org/code/eptw/profiles/72.html
www.bartonreading.com/early.html
www.lcps.k12.nm.us?Departments/FedPrograms/care_network.shtml

7

Evaluating Change

Jesse thought that maybe he could do this school thing after all. He just wasn't sure that he was ready to show it.

No one can alter someone else's attitudes and behaviors. What we can do is optimize the situation to encourage a student's self-reflection and provide an environment that is safe enough for student risk taking. We need to reflect on the enormity of our expectations—changes in long-held behaviors and attitudes—for the educators, parents, and students. It will be a scary adventure for all concerned. We humans tend to find comfort in the known, even if the known environment and behaviors are not working and are potentially harmful. As adults, we must model and operationalize the process of change. As adults, we must first admit that what we are doing currently isn't working for all of our kids. If it were, we wouldn't need this book and you wouldn't be reading it. We need to consciously abandon old comfortable practices and shove off into unknown waters. The good news is that these aren't uncharted waters. Others have succeeded before you. See, for example, the mission statement from Tucker Middle School in Figure 7.1.

Figure 7.1. The Tucker Pledge to Excellence

We, the teachers, students, and families of the Tucker School, pledge to be a community of learners. We believe that children learn from caring adults, adults learn from children, children learn from children, and adults learn from each other.

We believe that all children can reach high standards and can care about each other. We will not give up when learning is difficult. Each of us pledges to attain a personal best every day.

We believe that we can change the world.

Tucker School   Pamela A. Mason, Ed.D., Principal
Milton, Massachusetts   Joseph Dolan, Assistant Principal

Used with permission of Pamela A. Mason, Ed.D.

Success must be defined in terms of progress and small improvements. You will see only minute changes at first. Think about an attempt to lose weight. We gain weight over a period of time and it takes some time for the weight to be lost. Think of this plan as Weight Watchers for at-risk students—Achievement Watchers, if you will. Students didn't attain destructive and disengaged behaviors overnight. It takes a plan, a charting of progress, a mentor, support, and feedback (and lots of patience and good humor) to get them back on track.

The Plan

The plan should be collaboratively designed. Determine who should be involved. Parents? Other teachers? Administrators? Counselors? At minimum, the teacher and student should jointly design the plan to fit the individual student's needs. If it's attention span that we're reaching for, for example, what will help the student to pay attention? Will an attention buddy help? Moving of the seat? Frequent class movement? Don't try to solve every problem. Take one or two goals, define them, and create ways of realistically reaching and assessing them. Behaviors can be modified a bit at a time rather than attempting drastic change. Both the teacher and the student (and the parents and the administrators) need to know the plan and the steps to achieve the goals. Communication and a coordinated vision are essential. Dr. Bess Scott, a principal from Lincoln, Nebraska, writes an e-mail to her faculty every morning to keep herself and her faculty on track. Such comunications identify talking points and common focus among educational professionals.

Such discussions lead to fresh ideas and a sense of purposeful direction. Figure 7.2 shows an example.

Figure 7.2. Faculty E-mail Communication

Good Morning!

Effective Teachers
"In the in-depth study of the two schools (that used star teachers to turn around achievement dramatically), more than 50 factors that contributed directly or indirectly to creating a professional learning community were identified. For example, all the teachers focused on effort rather than ability as explanation for school success. The teachers saw effective instruction as a matter of life and death for their students. Moreover, the teachers expected to have problems as part of their daily work. They viewed working with English language–limited students and inclusion students as an integral, not an extra, part of their jobs. And they accepted accountability for student achievement." Notice how closely these examples correlate with Efficacy Concept #1! Teachers believe in the capacity of their students to learn, perform, and behave at grade level or above. (From "Can Star Teachers Create Learning Communities," by Martin Haberman, *Educational Leadership,* May 2004.)

Efficacy
"Smart is not something you are. Smart is something you get." We will spend the rest of the year examining and dissecting these four efficacy concepts. Let's continue with Efficacy Concept #2: Teachers know and are able to articulate to students and parents what grade level is. To get every student to learn, perform, and behave at grade level or above, students and their families must understand what grade level looks like. Once students and families understand what the target is, students must be taught the skills to reach the target. Students need to be reminded on a constant basis what their objective (the grade-level target) is so they understand why they are learning what they are learning. In *Classroom Instruction That Works,* Chapter 8, Robert Marzano addresses how and why to keep the objective in front of the student!

Effective Teams
(Trust, Embracing of Conflict, Commitment, Accountability,
Collective Results)

Let's start to think about how we eliminate each dysfunction one level
at a time. Think about your different teams and their qualities. This
week, I will list some concrete examples with which you can assess
yourself and your teams. "Members of teams with an absence of trust
dread meetings and find reasons to avoid spending time together.
Members of trusting teams look forward to meetings and other opportunities to work as a group." What "gut feeling" do you have when an-
ticipating a team meeting? How do your actions contribute? (From *The
Five Dysfunctions of a Team: A Leadership Fable,* by Patrick Lencioni,
Jossey-Bass, 2002.)

FISH (from the FISH! 2005 calendar)
"Be There: As you go about your day, notice where your thoughts go
when you are not present with people. What are you typically thinking
about? If your thoughts are not in the present moment, where are
they?"

Bess

Used with permission by Dr. Bess Scott, Principal, McPhee Elementary
School, Lincoln, NE.

Progress

We all need to see a bit of progress to keep at our tasks, so how can we
concretely chart student improvements?

- Note teacher absences and student absences. See if there are any
  patterns or changes.

- Look at the number of student trips to the nurse or counselor's office.

- Consider the number of office referrals. A goal should be the
  minimization of referrals.

- See if in-school suspensions and detentions decrease.

- Survey kids' attitudes often; compare and contrast the results.

- Talk with the parents—often. Call home with the positive as frequently or more frequently than with the negative. See if parents
  are noticing changes in attitudes (try to determine if parents' attitudes are changing).

- Notice kids' time on task. If a student is improving, note it and give feedback accordingly. (Carry around a clipboard with all of the students' names on it. If you observe a notable behavior, record it. Then, during regular student-teacher conferences, discuss your observations with the student.)

A Mentor

Effective Weight Watcher and Achievement Watcher leaders and mentors share common characteristics:

- They are nonjudgmental about past behaviors. What's done is done. We're only looking forward from here.
- They help you set attainable individual goals and concrete steps to reach them.
- They share tips for success and use some delicate self-disclosure.
- They seem to understand when you have a setback. Instead of getting angry, they encourage a better week next week and help you learn from your mistakes and get back on track.
- They encourage self-reflection and the recording of behaviors in a log or journal. They mark your progress and keep it confidential.
- They check on your progress regularly.
- They establish and maintain a community of support. However, an individual's success is not dependent on the group's success.
- They are positive and optimistic.
- They use encouraging language, humor, and enthusiasm.
- They encourage sharing among the group, understanding that they alone do not possess all the answers.
- They give you resources that will help you in your task and explain how they work.
- They seem genuinely glad when you show up—regardless of how your week has gone.
- They don't give up on you when or if you fail. They understand that it's a struggle and will support you unconditionally. They will help you (even though it's your decision) to determine your mistakes and redirect your actions.

Support

Support is always necessary for meaningful change to occur. Teachers must provide support for their students, and administrators must provide support for their teachers. The students, teachers, and school administrators must also perceive the community as supportive and caring.

Too often, teachers who assume the role of change agents are viewed harshly by their peers as "rocking the boat." Administrators need to make clear the expectation that rocking the boat is required. It's too difficult to work with disengaged students day in and day out only to have to justify your actions to disgruntled colleagues when the day is done. That's why the school climate must send the message that "this is a place where we work hard so all may achieve, and this meaningful work will most definitely cause some discomfort." We expect that discomfort and use it to inform our practice rather than ignore it and let it build.

Sometimes support needs to be in the form of staff development, but it does not necessarily have to be the traditional kind. Often the best support given is that of the resource of time. Instead of bringing a speaker in for an in-service day, how about some time to work as a staff to look at our needs and how we might best support each other and address these needs? Decide the following: What do we want to do? How are we going to do it? What do we need to get it done?

Do some reading of the professional literature. Use some time to check out the resources listed in this book. Have a collegial, focused discourse about the changes that need to be made. We recommend that those teachers with team planning time use at *least* one period a month to read and share professional reading.

Feedback

We all need feedback about our progress. At first it must come from someone else, usually our mentor. But if we want achievement and learning to be lifelong habits, we must show our students how to become self-evaluators and self-regulators.

Regular student-teacher conferences are invaluable. Many English teachers have known this for years. Some quality one-on-one time about a student's learning and challenges is time well spent. Take five minutes to check up on a student's progress, to reorient him or her, and to comment on effort. Make sure that students know what they're supposed to do and how they should approach the task. Rubrics are helpful not only for teachers' grading purposes, but also to point the student in the right direction (see Chapter 5).

Help students to set goals and make their plan. Use questions such as these to assist them:

- ◆ What is your goal?
- ◆ What mini-goals will help you be successful?
- ◆ What steps must you take to reach the first mini-goal?
- ◆ What strengths do you have to help you meet these goals?
- ◆ What challenges do you think you may face?
- ◆ How will you know if you're making progress?
- ◆ What can I do to help?
- ◆ What have you done to reach your mini-goal?
- ◆ What has worked and why did it work?
- ◆ What didn't work and why didn't it work?
- ◆ Do you need to restate any of your goals? Any steps?
- ◆ What will you do next?

Sample Student Survey Questions

- ◆ What motivates you?
- ◆ What can teachers do to help you learn the best?
- ◆ What concerns do you have about school?
- ◆ What concerns do you have about your own learning?
- ◆ What are you good at?

In addition, we recommend that you use the Search Institute's list of Developmental Assets to determine the needs of your individual students. The list is well researched and can indicate areas in need of improvement locally. The list can be found at the Search Institute's website at www.search-institute.org/assets/assetlists.html.

Conclusion

We will always be challenged by disenchanted and disengaged students. There is no miracle cure or process. We reach students one at a time by offering individual support and human compassion. We do not wipe our hands clean of a student simply because others have, including, perhaps, the parents. We do not worry about others who say that we're being naive or idealistic. If we don't set the bar high for ourselves, how can we ethically do so for our students? Instead of viewing our children as at risk, we'd like to suggest that we think of them as "at promise." When they say, "Teach me—I dare you," we answer, "Gladly."

Appendix

Interview Questions for Students Who Appear to be At- Risk

Tell me about your school.

Tell me about the best part of your school day.

Tell me about the worst part of your school day.

What do you like to do in your spare time?

Tell me about the kind of teacher you learn best from.

Have you ever been sent to the principal's office? Why?

What could teachers do to help you do well in school?

How do you feel about the other students in this school?

What is the easiest subject for you to learn and why?

What is the hardest subject for you to learn and why?

What are some things you would really like to learn?

How do you learn things?

What should the adults in this building know about this school?

Team Discussion Sheet for Student Recognition

Too often teams only take time to discuss the troubled students. When teams take time to discuss all their students, fewer students have difficulties in school. Use the following checklist to discuss at least ten students at each team meeting. These discussions should not last more than the time it takes to decide which category they fit into. This instrument is to make sure that all students are recognized for good work and for difficulties that they may be having.

Date:			
Team Members:	**Commendation or Recognition**	**Parent Contact Needed**	**Referral to?**
1.			
2.			
3.			
4.			
5.			
6.			
7.			
8.			
9.			
Etc.			

Sample Student Survey Questions

What motivates you?

What can teachers do to help you learn the best?

What concerns do you have about school?

What concerns do you have about your learning?

What are you good at?

What type of help could you use in school?

Student Information Sheet

Dear Parent:

The staff at our middle school is very interested in helping your child succeed in middle school. We would like you to fill out this information sheet which will be given to your child's homeroom/advisory teacher. The more information that you can give us about your child, his or her strengths or needs, and any concerns that you may have, the better we can plan the appropriate learning environment for each student. Thank you for your help.

Name of Student: _____

Name of Homeroom/Advisory Teacher: _____

Please identify your child's areas of strength:

Please identify any concerns you have about your child in school:

Please describe your child's learning patterns regarding organizational skills, homework style, etc.

In your opinion, what type of instructional approach helps your child to learn in the most effective manner?

Please describe your child's interests, hobbies, skills, etc. that may not always be evident in the classroom environment.

Please tell us any family or personal information that will help us know your child better.

What goals do you have for your child this year?

Student Self Assessment Instrument

Directions: Have each student complete the following questions at least once during the marking period. This is especially helpful right before the marking period is over. Use the information to have a one-on-one conference with the student.

Name_____

Subject: _____ Date: _____ Time: _____

Completion of my assignments (responsible worker):

_____ All of my assignments were turned in on time.

_____ Most of my assignments were turned in on time.

_____ I had _____ (number) late assignments.

You may check more than one choice about the quality of your work (quality producer).

So far this marking period I have done:

_____ High quality work   _____ Fair work

_____ Good work   _____ Not my best

My behavior this period has been: (check one)

_____ outstanding   _____ good _____ fair _____ poor

While working in groups I have (collaborative worker):

_____ done more than my share _____ done very little

_____ worked well with others _____ not worked well with others

With math partner:

_____ done more than my share _____ done very little

_____ worked well with others _____ not worked well with others

This marking period I was proud of:

_____

_____

Next marking period I will try to:

_____

_____

The most important thing I learned this marking period was:

_____

_____

Index